Praise for

Becoming Whole

Becoming Whole by Linda Myers is a thoughtful and important book for people dealing with upheavals in their lives. In a fascinating mix of cutting edge research and ancient wisdom, Myers makes a compelling case for the power of words as a form of healing and growth. This is a smart and heartfelt book.

—James W. Pennebaker, Ph.D., Professor of Psychology, The University of Texas at Austin and author of *Opening Up* and *Writing To Heal*

In *Becoming Whole*, Linda Joy Myers writes with great compassion and joy about the changes she sees in her students as they write their healing stories. This must-read book offers writers the safety and encouragement they need to mine the depths of their souls and reclaim their lives.

—Maureen Murdock, author of *Unreliable Truth: On Memoir and Memory* and *The Heroine's Journey: Woman's Quest for Wholeness*

Becoming Whole gently guides both fledgling and experienced writers through the process of unearthing one's past, transforming memories into memoir, and gaining the insight and understanding this process reveals. It is a wise and instructive book, full of practical tips and techniques for even the most timid writer. *Becoming Whole* reminds us that writing one's story not only affirms our unique life experiences, but also offers profound self-healing.

—Sharon Bray, Ed. D., author of *When Words Heal: Writing Through Cancer* and *A Healing Journey: Writing Together Through Breast Cancer*

Using her remarkable expertise as a therapist, author, and writing instructor, Linda Joy Myers gently advises and inspires anyone who wishes to use writing as a healing tool. *Becoming Whole* is profoundly encouraging; its instructions wise and specific. I recommend this book for anyone who wants to experience resolution, solace, and catharsis through writing.

—Michele Weldon, Assistant Professor of Journalism at Northwestern
University, and author of *Writing to Save Your Life*

Becoming Whole will give you a new perspective on the personal journey that is your life and serve as a healing, empowering guide as you explore the depth and breadth of your Self.

—Susan Albert, author of *Writing from Life: Telling Your Soul's Story*

Beautifully written and organized. Practical, inspired, accessible, and comprehensive, Myers' book gives you excellent tools to make writing a healing experience. Your story matters, and this book shows you why.

—John Fox, author of *Poetic Medicine: The Healing Art of Poem-making*

That writing can help us explore and articulate our pain, losses, and perplexities is a widely accepted idea, but how to go about writing effective healing narratives is hardly self-explanatory. Linda Myers has provided a lively, most helpful guidebook for memoirists setting out on their journeys of recollection and recovery. The practical advice and exercises are accompanied by a wonderful range of anecdotes that serve not only to entertain but also to model the kind of writing her readers may hope to achieve. A valuable addition to the literature of self-exploration.

—Marilyn Chandler, Ph.D., author, *A Healing Art*; board member,
Center for Medicine, Humanities, and Law, UC Berkeley

Linda Joy Myers not only shows writers how to start and sustain a life-long writing practice, but in her wise, tender, and clear book, she also models the kind of courage necessary to enlarge the creative spirit. Cultivating such courage makes both our writing and living more meaningful, vibrant, and free.

—Caryn Mirriam-Goldberg, Ph.D., author of *Write Where You Are*
and founder of Transformative Language Arts at Goddard College

This compelling and wise book shows you how to listen to your inner voice and uncover the important stories in your life. Myers provides a process that leads you to transformation and healing. If you've ever had a notion about writing a memoir, read this book!

—Lee Glickstein, founder of Transformational Speaking Circles and author of *Be Heard Now!*

What a wonderful, well-written, engaging book. With its combination of practical information, engrossing stories, and focused writing exercises, it is an excellent adjunct to psychotherapy and EMDR. I will recommend *Becoming Whole: Writing Your Healing Story* to my clients and colleagues.

—Laurel Parnell, Ph.D., author of *Transforming Trauma: EMDR* and *EMDR in the Treatment of Adults Abused as Children*

Linda Myers draws upon her many roles and perspectives—as person, as therapist, as writer, and as teacher in *Becoming Whole*. Artfully weaving together these views, she has produced a work that should prove a gentle and helpful guide to those who wish to write their own stories.

—Joshua Smyth, Ph.D.

Also by Linda Joy Myers

Don't Call Me Mother: Breaking the Chain of Mother–Daughter Abandonment

Becoming Whole

Writing Your Healing Story

Linda Joy Myers, Ph.D.

IASO BOOKS
A Division of
Two Bridges Press
www.twobridgespress.com

Iaso Books
A Division of Two Bridges Press
1700 Solano Ave
Berkeley, CA. 94707
www.twobridgespress.com

Originally published in a different form by Silver Threads, San Diego.

Manufactured in the United States of America

Designed by Studio P

Cover Artwork by Linda Joy Myers
Text editing by Mindy Toomay and Lisa A. Smith

Library of Congress Control Number: 2007928864

ISBN-13: 978-0-9793061-3-6
ISBN-10: 0-9793061-3-2

FIRST REVISED EDITION

Table of Contents

Foreword

There is a healing power in the very writing of our stories, whether they are read by others or not. In the years since I began doing life story workshops in 1988, I have witnessed many times how this writing brings peace and resolution to writers who have been tormented and undermined by stories they have kept within them.

I am not the only one to take stock of this. Many times, my workshop attendees have said to me, "This is like therapy, but it costs a lot less and it's a whole lot more fun."

"As I wrote my autobiography," one woman said, "it became obvious that something was happening to me. I was feeling a peace with my life that I had not felt prior to writing. As I continued to write, I felt more and more acceptance and consolation."

As Linda Joy Myers explains so clearly in the following pages, the writing of a life story creates an observer self whose empathetic listening presence brings validation and acceptance to the writer. And as James Pennebaker has demonstrated over the years with various study groups, it is in the writing of the story even more than in the speaking that this healing occurs.

I have always felt that this was so because in the speaking the story remains evanescent, easily lost, enduring somehow only as long as the memory of the hearer endures. As such, speaking a memory offers little consolation to the speaker that his or her memory will last as a witness to what was lived. When a story is written, however, its memory has the promise of survival that is as long as the writing itself.

Healing is a process of becoming whole. And people cannot become whole until they know how and where their existence fits into the human experience. Otherwise they are left with the question, "Why?" Writing life stories is an important personal experience because it can answer the "why?" In the past, people sat with their families and told them stories, perhaps sitting in their kitchen rockers around the fireplace or woodstove. There the old people told stories of their youth and their parents' lives, and the children took the stories in even if sometimes only by osmosis, sometimes without even listening carefully. And the stories became part of the way families thought about themselves and interpreted their experience.

Now, however, with families scattered all around the country and the world, it has become increasingly difficult to tell these stories because too often there is no one to hear them. The storyteller who now wishes to tell the family stories has to put them in writing and disseminate them to the family in printed form. A different way of telling a story but an effective way. And one that brings healing.

Today, more than ever before, people are writing their stories to celebrate their lives and to create a way to break through the silence that envelops us all. Now, Linda Joy Myers has written a readable book in which she brings to the topic of life writing as a healing art her years of psychotherapeutic experience coupled with her training and experience as a writer and teacher.

I am proud to say that she has been part of our Soleil Lifestory Network since 1998, teaching people to write personal and family stories. During that time, I have talked with her often about her work and have witnessed her dedication and commitment to bringing the art of life writing not only to the therapeutic community but to the average person who may never have thought of himself or herself as a writer.

The beauty of this book is that it not only explains why the process works but shows the reader how to make the process work in his or her life. This book deserves to have a wide readership and to know a long success. It offers an important access to healing.

Denis Ledoux
Soleil Lifestory Network
Lisbon Falls, Maine

Acknowledgements

or support, encouragement, and generous giving of time to talk about ideas and read drafts, I thank Doreen Hamilton. To my teacher and mentor Ron Kane, who has shown me a healing path for twenty-five years, heartfelt thanks for his vision, his steadfast compassion, and most of all, for his fierce belief in healing and transformation.

Denis Ledoux has encouraged my memoir teaching and writing for several years; his passion and love for memoir has been an inspiration and a guiding light. The new edition of this book has come to life thanks to the superb editing and mentoring by Mindy Toomay and Lisa A. Smith.

I am grateful to James Pennebaker, Joshua Smyth, Sharon Bray, Maureen Murdock, Michele Weldon, Laurell Parnell, Susan Albert, Caryn Mirriam Goldberg, John Fox, and Marilyn Chandler for their work, and their belief in the healing power of writing.

My children, Theron, Amanda, and Shannon, have shown me that change and healing can pass to the next generation, and I celebrate a new generation of much loved grandchildren: Miles, Zoe, and Seth. My deep gratitude goes to my children for their love and generosity as we weave new stories in the family.

I thank all my students and workshop participants for sharing their stories with me, and showing me over the years how the writing process is healing for them, and how it transforms their lives. My work in using the earlier editions of this book to spread the word about writing and healing has been supported and enhanced by several writing organizations: The California Writers Club, The

Women's National Book Association, and the National Association for Poetry Therapy.

Story Circle Network has continued to support memoir as a healing process through the years, and has given me many opportunities to share my work.

Thank you.

Introduction

I began learning about autobiography lying in a featherbed with my great-grandmother Blanche when I was eight years old. We nestled in the soft down and watched the lights from the highway flicker across the ceiling. Silver moonlight fell on white cotton sheets that smelled of the sun. A mile to the east, the Mississippi River flowed by. Blanche's house stood on The Island, a wedge of land bordered by the river and a slough, where our family had lived for five generations. Blanche was in her eighties then and seemed an ancient relic, with great folds and wrinkles and deeply etched eyes. During the day she fiercely hoed the weeds that threatened her garden, occasionally popping a fresh strawberry into my mouth. She used a wood stove for all her cooking and taught me how to listen to the roar of the fire to know when it was hot enough to bake our apple pie.

During those nights in the featherbed, her teeth in a jelly jar on the nightstand, she murmured the stories of her life—how she was an adult before the telephone and radio were invented; how she delivered the family farm's milk, eggs, and butter by horse and wagon to town seven miles away. I learned that she'd married her first husband, Lewis, on New Year's Day in 1894. He died of pneumonia in March, unaware that Blanche was pregnant. Sixty years later, his death was still mourned by Blanche and her daughter, my grandmother, Lulu. The tears they both shed sixty years after his death showed me the power of history and that stories explain how things come to be the way they are.

I was raised by my grandmother rather than my mother. By age seven I'd witnessed many intense conflicts between these two women that scared and confused me. Blanche was the mother of the mother of my mother, and knew the history that trailed behind them like smoke. Night after night during every summer of my childhood, we lay in that featherbed and Blanche told me the family stories. It would be years, however, before I knew that Josephine had been raised mostly by Blanche's mother.

All these women are dead now. The focus of my adult life has been to heal the wounds that were passed down from them. After growing up with so many power struggles and grudges, I was determined to break the pattern. I always wondered how people came to healing and forgiveness, how they found their way back to love despite deep injuries. These questions about love and healing became the focus of a lifelong quest. I tell that story in my memoir *Don't Call Me Mother: Breaking the Chain of Mother-Daughter Abandonment.*

In my thirties, I earned a master's degree and became a therapist, after many years of being in therapy myself. Throughout my healing process I used writing—a journal, diaries, and stories—to tell and retell the family stories of abuse, abandonment, and what I came to learn was mental illness in our family. I had always wanted to "really" write, to go beyond the journal and write our story in full. So in 1993 I stopped teaching family therapy and joined the Mills College Creative Writing Program, where I received my M.F.A. There I learned the skills and techniques I needed to shape my story into a book.

Over the years, I explored the ideas of body healing, emotional healing, and healing in the deepest layers of the soul. Eventually I came upon the writing-as-healing research of James Pennebaker, Ph.D., and his colleagues. I was excited to find studies that prove what many of us have known intuitively—that writing helps to heal the body as well as the mind, and perhaps even the soul. Pennebaker's books and research, and a new generation of studies that appear in *The Writing Cure,* edited by Stephen Lepore and Joshua Smyth, prove how much writing true, authentic stories can heal us on all these levels.

As a memoir coach—face-to-face in Berkeley, California or on-line—I am moved and inspired by the stories I hear about how healing the writing experience is for my students. Their stories are written one vignette at a time, and then quilted together into a whole, healing story. They come to writing with humility, curiosity, and determination, and—as with all creative endeavors—they have to persevere through the hard times when the writing doesn't flow. They must confront their feelings as well as their family histories as they cultivate ever greater commitment to the work. It has been a joy to teach these students and to receive their stories, some of which appear in these pages.

In this book you will learn how writing can be used to heal your pain, both physical and emotional. Don't postpone this liberating process. Start writing your own true story, today.

Linda Joy Myers

Healing through Memoir Writing

We shall not cease from exploration
And the end of all our exploring
Will be to arrive where we started
And know the place for the first time.

—T. S. Eliot

1

The Courage to be a "Real" Writer

> *. . . the same immense energies that create the symptoms of trauma, when properly engaged and mobilized, can transform the trauma and propel us into new heights of healing, mastery, and even wisdom.*
>
> —Peter Levine, *Waking the Tiger: Healing Trauma*

*I*n the course of my work as a memoir coach, I have met countless people who have a passion to write. If we are to live that passion, we must conquer a fierce internal adversary: the critic who admonishes us to use perfect grammar and eloquent language, and convinces us that if we were "real" writers the writing would flow effortlessly.

In my workshops, we talk about what a "real" writer is: someone who is published, polished, and vetted by the New York establishment; someone super-confident who writes twenty pages a day without confronting any obstacles. But the truth is that all writers, even famous ones, struggle with internal critical voices.

The critical voice may suggest that you are boring, or that your words and ideas will be a burden to the world. It often says such things as, "Why bother, who cares, what makes you think that anything you have to say is important?" If you have a "writing wound" caused by having had your creative efforts minimized or ridiculed, trying to write may feel like a battle, often a ferocious battle, fought between the part that wants to write and the part that criticizes. So it takes extra effort to encourage our creativity, to invite it to come out of hiding.

There is another task that stands in the way for many would-be memoir writers. They must learn to ignore an inner voice that shouts: "Don't write that story, you'll shame us. We'll never speak to you again!" Many people are haunted by unspoken rules forbidding them from exposing the family's dirty laundry. Because of these old scripts, writers become afraid to unleash their authentic voices and speak their own truths.

Often we feel the need to present ourselves and our families in the best light. This is not necessarily wrong. In fact, for people who tend to focus on the negative, this "best light" method can be quite healing. But those who are ashamed or who feel cowed by the old family code of silence must tell their deeply honest stories in order to heal. If you are such a person, your inner critic may tap into your fear, shame, and doubt to keep you silent. You must give yourself permission to tell the truth. I will discuss the inner critic and how to deal with truth telling in memoir writing in later chapters.

In my writing workshops, I have seen amazing breakthroughs. Perhaps the safety and support of the group catch the inner critic unawares. Or perhaps the intense passion of the writer is ignited by the group process, inviting the stories to emerge.

The people who attend my workshops often gasp at the beauty and courage of vignettes written in a few short minutes. These snapshots of a much larger story astonish us because they are fresh and real, composed in an atmosphere of trust. Each vignette piques our curiosity as the weeks pass, because it sheds light on the whole person we are getting to know through her weekly stories.

One woman wrote a character sketch about her young son, a beautiful golden boy of eight, who is the center of her life. She wrote and read about how important he is to her, coming into her life after she thought she would never have children. She wrote about the joy he has given her and grieved for the years when she was in despair about having no children. The group witnessed and held her in respectful, embracing silence. Kleenex was passed silently from hand to hand as everyone received her story. The room was filled with compassion and support, which she could feel and receive. She looked at us and wiped her eyes.

"Wow. I guess I took up a lot of time. I'm sorry."

Everyone began murmuring, telling her how deeply the story had affected them, reflecting back to her what she had written and lived. As she was witnessed by the group, she began to relax and smile. Eventually she said, "I've never told anyone all this. I have never had the space to do this before."

The healing this student experienced was not only in the writing of her story but in the sharing of what had been private. Later she wrote to me: "Attending this workshop was my gift to myself. It gave me the opportunity to reach deep inside myself, draw a circle of words around my heart, and share my deepest feelings with a group of fellow writers who were there waiting to receive me and hold me with compassion and acceptance. I left the workshop feeling fuller and more whole."

The National Association for Poetry Therapy, a group dedicated to using writing and literature for healing, stresses the importance of groups for writers. The association suggests that there are three important stages of the writing-as-healing process:

1. Writing

2. Reading your writing to yourself

3. Sharing the work with others and being witnessed

The title "writer" can be intimidating. I have met many people whose writing is poetic and wonderful, but they wouldn't call themselves writers. "I don't identify with 'writer.' It isn't really me." Many of us get caught up in identity and labels.

Writing is simply an activity. If you write, you are a writer. Invite yourself to dip into the flow of words in your head and write down what you hear. You will be amazed at what you have to say, at the wisdom that resides within you just waiting to be tapped as you record and share your unique story.

Brenda Ueland, in her wonderful classic *If You Want to Write*, says that everyone is talented and original. All of us need to share our ideas with the world; it is part of our right as human beings to express ourselves. Ueland says that criticism destroys creativity. So-called helpful criticism is often the worst kind.

Whenever I got discouraged about writing, I would read and reread Ueland's book. It is full of wisdom and a positive spirit about our deep, inner creativity. She says we must write freely, as if to friends who appreciate us and find us interesting. We should write as if they are saying to us, "Tell me more, tell me all you can. I want to understand more about everything you feel and know and all the changes inside and out of you. Let more come out."

If you want to write, think about how you can create space for writing in your life, a time and a place where you can nurture this spark into a roaring blaze. As you write, think of yourself as a listener, a translator. Focus inward and hear the stories that whisper to you in a low key; tune into your desire to capture your grandmother's history, your mother's face, or your father's character. The creative spark lives in everyone—all you need to do is feed the flame.

And keep going, despite whatever difficulty arises. Even after completing two books, I continue to wrestle with words, phrases, and internal permission to write my truth. I have to force myself to sit down and write. We must all do this dance as we unfurl our stories onto paper.

Writing Invitations

1. Name five reasons you want to write your life stories.

2. Write about what being a "real" writer means to you.

3. What support do you have in your life to write?

4. What stories do you like to read? Have these helped to heal you?

5. Describe the town, city, landscape you grew up in. Include buildings, weather, your favorite things about this place.

6. How did the place where you grew up shape you into the person you are today?

7. What family story that you heard as a child excites you or captures your interest? Write that story.

8. Record what the critic voices have to say—the voices that stop or discourage you. We will spend more time on the critic later.

2

Writing and Healing

*One can enjoy the health benefits of writing without the
emotional costs associated with writing about trauma. The
physical benefits of writing about one's best possible self were
equal to or better than writing about trauma.*

—Laurie King

*W*riting your true story can heal you, both physically and
emotionally. Expressive writing, writing that integrates
your emotions and insights with memories of events
that occurred in your past, has been shown to improve the immune
system and have a positive effect on such diseases as chronic fatigue
syndrome, arthritis, and asthma.

Self-disclosure and confession have long played a role in reliev-
ing stress and promoting health. As an ancient church sacrament,
confession ritualizes the unburdening of shame and guilt, enabling
a person to move forward in a positive way. In the closed privacy
of this ritual, words are found to speak the unspeakable—halting
sentences woven through with shame and guilt, grief and regret.
These words pierce through the inner darkness, opening our hearts
to the light of hope and forgiveness. Through confession and
unburdening, forgiveness can begin, for ourselves and others.

Psychotherapy has been called the modern day confessional.
Freud positioned himself in the shadows of a dimly lit room—a
sacred, private space in which clients could reveal hidden truths.

His treatment rule was that they were to speak freely about whatever arose in their minds. This was a revolutionary, even dangerous, idea in Victorian times, when repression and suppression of thoughts and desires were the order of the day. In therapy, as in the church ritual of confession, deep feelings, worries, and the secrets of the soul could finally be formed into words.

During the 1990s, Dr. James Pennebaker, a psychologist at the University of Texas, began to wonder if writing would offer the same relief as spoken disclosure. For a decade, he and his colleagues investigated the therapeutic benefit of writing in various settings and with a large range of populations, including prisoners and crime victims, arthritis and chronic-pain sufferers, new mothers, and people with various physical illnesses, across different social classes and demographics.

During one such experiment, members of the control group were instructed to write lists or plans for the day, while the expressive writing group received the following directions:

For the next four days, I would like you to write about your very deepest thoughts and feelings about the most traumatic experience of your entire life. In your writing, I'd like you to really let go and explore your very deepest emotions and thoughts. You might tie your topic to your relationships with others, including parents, lovers, friends, or relatives; to your past, your present, or your future; or to who you have been, who you would like to be, or who you are now. You may write about the same general issues or experiences on all days of writing or on different traumas each day. All of your writing will be completely confidential.

Both groups wrote for fifteen minutes on each of the four days of the study.

Even though Dr. Pennebaker is a psychologist, the intensity and depth of the trauma expressed in the subjects' stories impressed and surprised him. Students wrote about tragic and traumatic events, such as depression, rape, suicide attempts, child sexual and physical abuse, drug use, and family violence. They wrote about powerful emotions associated with these stories, which often elicited tears, yet most were willing to participate in the study again.

The researchers found that it is indeed healing to translate our experiences into words, to put events and feelings into perspective using written language.

In *Opening Up: The Healing Power of Expressing Emotions*, Pennebaker discusses how writing about emotional events relieves stress and promotes a more complete understanding of events. He concludes that simple catharsis, the explosive release of emotions, is not enough. Feelings, thoughts, and a new comprehension need to be integrated in our minds with memories of the events that occurred in order to create a new perspective. Pennebaker compares the effects of writing to psychotherapy, where emotional disclosure and the release of inhibition are part of the healing process, along with the ability to integrate new insights into current behavior and beliefs.

As far back as Wilhelm Reich (1897–1957) psychologists have suggested that repression and suppression of emotion contribute to stress and emotional and physical imbalance. In a primitive fight-or-flight system, powerful chemicals surge through the body to protect an organism against a perceived threat. When the threat, or stressor, has passed, the body can retain the pattern of tension and vigilance, especially if there has been ongoing or severe trauma. When stress is released, the immune system responds in a positive direction, toward balance and ultimate health.

In 1999, an article by Joshua Smyth et al. in the Journal of the American Medical Association about the effects of expressive writing on arthritis and asthma sufferers made a rousing splash in the writing and psychological communities. In their 2002 book *The Writing Cure*, Smyth and Stephen Lepore present more recent studies showing that while writing about trauma and negative emotions causes emotional pain and distress for a short period, both mood and physical health improve. Furthermore, writing about positive emotions and a positive future also lead to improvements in physical as well as emotional health.

The research also showed that our personalities affect these benefits. If a person tends to withhold emotions, writing about negative experiences will likely have a positive effect on that person's health. If a person generally focuses on negative feelings, writing about a positive experience or a happier life event may have a beneficial effect. Therefore, there is no single "right" way to use writing as a healing tool.

As research about the healing aspects of writing continues, we learn more and more about how to write ourselves well. Here is what one of my students, Clare Cooper Marcus, wrote about her experience with writing as a healing practice:

> *I'm lucky—writing comes easily to me. Between the ages of five and eleven, I attended a small country school run by five eccentric women who insisted that we all write at least one essay a week. It was assumed that we all could write, and we did.*
>
> *Fifty years later, my body and emotions thrown into turmoil by a diagnosis of breast cancer, it seemed the most natural thing in the world to record my feelings in a journal. I wrote while sitting, wracked with anxiety, in the hospital waiting room. I wrote about my fear of death, of pain, of not-knowing. I wrote sitting up in bed after my mastectomy, I wrote in the hospital garden, drinking in nurturance from the hundred-year-old Valley Oak tree, the squirrels running up its rotted trunk. I was writing myself into hope.*
>
> *Writing was for me a form of Zen practice. It helped me stay in the present moment, aware of each feeling and insight arising, then falling away, like leaves drifting by on a stream of consciousness. Writing at such a time was an exercise in mindfulness. Although I also spoke my feelings out loud, to friends, to a therapist, to members of a support group, it was writing that enabled me to go deeper, to give my soul a voice. I believe it was writing as much as medical treatment that enabled me to heal.*

Writing Yourself Well Techniques

In his research, Pennebaker found that when subjects used a large number of positive words (happy, good, laugh) along with a moderate number of negative words (angry, hurt, ugly) in their writing, health improvements were likely. Cognitive or thinking words (because, reason, effect) and words of self-reflection (I understand, realize, know) created the most resolution. So if you want to experience the greatest healing benefit from your writing, pay attention to the emotional content of your words, and keep writing about a particular memory until you have causally linked the events with your feelings.

Causality occurs when an action or other stimulus leads to an outcome: This happened because that happened first. There is no causal linkage between the two events in the following sentence: *The queen died. The king died.* But in the next example, you can see a connection: *The queen died. The king died of grief.*

Your first efforts at writing memoir may be filled with confusion and negative or unintegrated emotions. Write an emotionally difficult story several times in different ways. After a while, you may find yourself writing from a positive perspective—telling, for instance, what you learned from the event, or how a negative experience made you change your life in a positive way. This furthers your process of self-understanding and healing.

Writing emotionally rich and integrated stories:

- Makes thoughts and events more concrete
- Leads to greater self-knowledge
- Releases emotional constriction and stress
- Strengthens the immune system
- Leads to short-term changes in the autonomic nervous system
- Provides a template for the writer's future story

Think about the stories in your life that connect into a meaningful whole. What do you need to do now to bring together the frayed threads of your life? Could these secret stories free you from the trap of silence?

Writing does not need to be difficult or complicated. Think of it as talking on paper, as Michele Weldon, author of *Writing to Save Your Life*, suggests. She goes on to say, "When you are writing to save your life, your feelings must be uncensored, raw, and unfiltered by the fear of reception. No one is judging you. No one else has to read what you have written. You are writing to save your life."

Give yourself permission to speak, to find your voice, to write. Let yourself enter new and unexplored territory. For twenty minutes, write a story you have never put into words before. Afterward, journal about how you felt writing it, and your reaction to seeing it in words.

Write into acceptance, support, and encouragement. Let your voice be heard.

Writing Invitations

1. Think about an important event in your life that led directly to another important event or to a person coming into your life. For instance, if you hadn't gone to the game that January night, you wouldn't have met John, whom you dated and eventually married. Write about what led up to this turning point in your life—the causal factors in this story.

2. Set your timer and write for ten minutes about a traumatic event, looking for an understanding, a causal meaning to that event that doesn't create self-blame. For instance, if you think you were raped because you wore a short skirt, that is self-blame. But if you realize that you didn't pay attention to your intuition and take a safer route home, that is an insight that can lead you to take better care of yourself in the future. Perhaps you didn't hear footsteps behind you because you were upset, you just had a fight with a friend, or you were sick. Integrating what happened into your overall understanding of yourself and the world can help you live your current life with more freedom and happiness.

3. Write about your best future self: Who will you be in one year? Five years? Imagine yourself living as you want to, but based on some aspect of reality and real possibilities that might emerge from who you are now.

4. Make a list of positive, healing words that make you feel good.

5. Write about an unexpected way in which you were blessed with healing, such as an experience with an animal or a garden.

3

Journals, Diaries, and Poetry

The diarist writes from an ever-moving present.
Autobiographic writing is written from a later point
in time, in retrospect.

—Tristine Rainer

Some of us started writing in diaries or journals as children. Then, as now, we poured out our most private thoughts and feelings there. You might have been lucky enough to have a secret place where you could hide your diary away from prying eyes. Or, perhaps you had no privacy, or your family believed that putting feelings or thoughts into words was dangerous or threatening.

When I was thirteen I received a diary with a little key, but I knew the key would not protect me. I found that diary recently, and I had to translate the words—jottings about events—into what I remembered was really going on beneath them. I had to keep my real thoughts and feelings secret even in my diary, because my ever intrusive grandmother would have too much of me if she read it—and I knew she would read it. I knew early on that the written word could cause lots of problems.

With a background like that, how did I ever become a writer?

I always loved stories and books, letters, and all kinds of writing. As I mentioned before, it was my great-grandmother Blanche and her stories, as well as my curiosity about our family history, that brought me to writing. Despite an inauspicious beginning with diary writing, I found that later in life I clung to my journal as if it were a raft about to take me over Niagara Falls.

Well, a raft might not help under those circumstances, but the journal helped me sort out confusion about my family, being rejected by my mother, and my grandmother's anger. Though these events happened when I was a child, their effect did not magically go away in adulthood. My journal provided me with a place to use my voice when I didn't have one in the world.

Putting the Truth on the Page

Because various members of my family invented their own versions of reality, I became obsessed with what was real and what was not, and I used my journal to record what really happened. I wrote about my hopes for a better life and my dreams about the future. I kept track of my night dreams, which showed me my unconscious thoughts, desires, and traumas. This tracking of my unconscious helped in my long-term healing process.

One exercise in the first major therapy group I attended included writing hundreds of pages of painful and negative stories from the past. We had to structure our writing into a story. We had to write what happened (events) and our reactions (feelings) about what happened. We were taught visualization so we could see how we looked and what we felt in younger versions of ourselves. Writing as if in a trance forced us to encounter mental and emotional states that we had tried, unsuccessfully, to bury in the depths of our unconscious.

These techniques helped bring back memories, including specific words and dialogue to make the past real. All of us in the group had found ourselves caught up in repeating the past, despite every prayer that we would not. That repetition is what brought us humbly to the therapy process, where writing helped to wake us up.

Kathleen Adams, president of the National Association for Poetry Therapy, has written several books about journal writing: *The Way of the Journal, The Write Way to Wellness*, and *Journal to the Self.* Throughout her life she has been dedicated to the process of healing through journal writing. As a counselor and experienced journal writer, she has learned various techniques, such as Ira Progoff's Intensive Journal method, that bring structure and logic to the process of journal writing. Through her training as well as her own experience, she realized that people bring different needs to their journal writing.

Adams developed structured exercises to help create a safe and measured way to enter into potentially painful material. She suggests that we be careful when writing about very traumatic experiences because the writing itself can be overwhelming and cause more stress, and that containment, relaxation, and nurturing help to bring a person back to balance.

If you want to know more about her suggestions for journal writing and healing, read her books and visit her website at www.journaltherapy.com.

Journal Writing Techniques

Many kinds of journal writing can have a healing effect.

• A daily diary keeps us in the present and allows us to track our activities, feelings, and tasks. This is a way to stay in the here and now, and to structure time, feelings, and goals through writing.

• Writing letters that will never be sent is a way to express your feelings to particular people without blasting them in real life with the force of your emotions. The unsent letter may be written to anyone, dead or alive, as a way to express perhaps forbidden or secret thoughts and feelings.

• Writing about your present and future selves and dialoguing with past selves—the person you were in earlier decades of your life—allow you to explore your identity: who you were, who you are, and who you are becoming.

A freewrite is a style of journal writing in which the pen does not come off the page for fifteen or twenty minutes. The unconscious is given full rein to ignore boundaries or interference by logic or a critic. In *Becoming a Writer*, Dorothea Brande says that "to have the full benefit of the richness of the unconscious, you must learn to write easily and smoothly when the unconscious is in the ascendant." She suggests that you should write the minute you wake up.

In my memoir groups we do a freewrite at the beginning of class. New stories and thoughts arise in the moment, and what comes out of the freewrite is often a surprise. New ideas seem to come from nowhere to find their way onto the page. Sometimes a certain problem with a scene or memory is solved during freewriting. It is a time to let go, a time to put the intellect aside and just write.

Inspiring books about journal writing include *Life's Companion* by Christina Baldwin, *The Artist's Way* by Julia Cameron, *Writing for Your Life* by Deena Metzger, *If You Want to Write* by Brenda Ueland, and, of course, *Becoming a Writer* by Dorothea Brande. These books feed my soul and help me keep writing when I hit a dry spot. Even as you craft stories for your memoir, journal writing and freewriting help you to heal and to keep your self-expression fluid and fresh.

Poetry as Autobiography

As many children do, I began writing poetry when I was young. My grandmother used to read to me from the *Oxford Book of English Verse*. One autumn night when I was nine years old, I sat next to her on the floor while she read "Annabel Lee," the cadence of the words sweeping us up together into a world of tragedy and love. She introduced me to Wordsworth, Longfellow, Carl Sandberg, the Brownings, and other traditional poets.

At age ten, in the heat of grief when a beloved cottonwood tree was cut down, I wrote my first poem, in which I poured out my sorrow about the tree's murder and my confusion about the adults' silence regarding this horrible event. I was a witness to this injustice, capturing the beauty and meaning of the tree in a few words.

Throughout my life poetry has lifted me from the depths of despair, especially e. e. cummings' poems in my twenties. I would copy his quirky and delightful poetry on cards and put them throughout the house, where they cheered me from despair and gave me hope.

For the darker times, I read Adrienne Rich, Denise Levertov, and T. S Eliot, searching for ways to make sense of my world and my feelings. At the first meeting of my poetry class at Mills College, I told my teacher, Marilyn Chandler, that poetry had saved my life, and she asked the other students if that had happened to them too. Many hands went up in acknowledgement of the power of poetry to heal.

When I began to write my autobiography, I did it through poetry, painting a picture of my family, my great-grandmother, my mother, my grandmother's death, and the grief I always felt because my mother denied me. I took poetry workshops and studied with Galway Kinnell, Lucille Clifton, and other poets at the Squaw Valley Poetry Workshop.

Finally, I gathered my poems, self-published them in a chapbook, and read them at poetry readings. But after a while I felt I had to write my autobiography in prose. A narrative would connect all the dots and would allow me to paint a more detailed picture of my feelings and experiences. I began a fictionalized version, which turned into a full-blown memoir.

Poetry allows us to capture fragments of insight and emotion because it does not depend on whole sentences or complete thoughts. A poem is a snapshot of a single moment, and in this moment all is contained within. In his book *Poetic Medicine*, John Fox says:

"Poetry provides guidance, revealing what you did not know you knew before you wrote the poem. This moment of surprising yourself with your own words or wisdom is at the heart of poetry as healer."

Beginning a Journal

You can have fun with your journal—it does not have to be deadly serious. Think about what surprises you in your life. What kind of relationship do you have with words, songs, and images? What rhythms get you up on your feet? Give yourself permission to play with words, and write daily in your journal.

If you are a beginner or have let your journal go, buy a new one. Allow yourself to choose one that gives you pleasure with the color of its cover or the smell of its leather.

How you choose to write—in pen or pencil, in wire-bound notebooks or leather-bound journals, or on the computer—does not matter. What is important is to listen to your inner voice and give yourself permission to say what you think. Play with words; create images and stories that give meaning and joy to your life. Pick up your pen and listen.

Writing Invitations

1. Select a group of words at random and write spontaneous poetry sparked by the ideas they provoke.

2. Write about a troubling event for 15 minutes. Consider how this event may have helped you make changes in your life or how it created new opportunities for you. In this vignette, tell what happened as well as your feelings about the event.

3. How do you feel now, after writing about that event? If you are upset, write about those feelings until you feel better. Then do something to nurture yourself.

4. Write about a positive experience. Think about moments when you felt whole, ecstatic, spiritually moved, or deeply loved. Consider experiences with nature, gardens, and animals.

5. Write what is called an "unsent letter" to a person with whom you have unfinished business, such as anger, grief, or regret. Set a timer and keep the writing short, 10 to 15 minutes for this first letter. Do not send the letter, but don't discard it. Later in the week write another version of this letter, and put it aside as well. In a month, read both letters and write a third version. Notice if you feel better or different about the person, the situation, or yourself.

4

Memories: The Good, the Bad, the Dangerous

*All sorrows can be borne if you put them into a story
or tell a story about them.*

—Isak Dinesen

Memories are woven deeply into the fabric of our lives. They help us know who we are; they help define us. Yet are we only what we remember? What about the memories that come up as we write and explore our deepest selves? Some memoirists have asked for my help with this subject. They begin their memoirs with enthusiasm and energy, looking forward to getting their stories on the page and discovering how the past has affected the present. But as the past is stimulated into current time by writing, new memories may come up, some of them painful. Sometimes we have unknowingly repressed our traumatic memories.

If traumatic memories gain a grip on your psyche, you may feel stuck, wanting to go forward, yet caught in the past. The solution: write yourself forward. Write yourself out of the stuck place.

Too often, memoir writers are chastised by family and society for not simply letting go of the past. "Get on with life; quit thinking about the past," they say. But people can't simply will themselves to forget what resides within. Sometimes memories intrude upon the psyche, as if demanding to be heard. Bad memories or parts of our pasts that are unresolved, have a way of intruding into our lives, as if demanding us to do our healing work.

When past memories are pleasing, the writing often comes easily and offers a positive foundation and a new perspective. Memories of traumatic events, however, can be as painful as the events themselves. The trauma of abuse, loss, or accidents affects the brain. A series of powerful chemical-physiological and emotional reactions accompany such memories. Psychiatrists and other clinicians use the term "Post-traumatic Stress Disorder" or PTSD to describe this state, which is now a common focus of treatment.

Continuing to write helps to resolve emotional issues by getting the images, feelings and conflicts out of us and onto the page, where they can be processed with more objectivity. In other words, the healing process is the writing itself.

Healing Trauma

When Dr. Pennebaker asked people to write about painful experiences, some of the stories that emerged related to traumas resulting from events in the outside world—natural disasters, car accidents, rape, or war. Others had to do with trauma or abuse at home—physical, emotional, and sexual abuse; alcoholism; and mental illness—abuse and trauma inflicted within what is supposed to be a safe place, at home and within the fabric of family and friends. That kind of injury is all the more insidious because the victims, particularly when they are children, don't realize that what is happening is wrong. It is simply the way mommy and daddy act. It's the way things are.

Even mature adults may feel that nothing can be done about life not being as they wish it to be. A pattern called "learned helplessness" describes those who feel stuck and unable to take action to change their lives. This is an unfortunate term that has been used derogatorily in reference to women. It is not actually helplessness that is learned, but a pattern of fear and immobilization resulting from trauma. This complex physiological and psychological reaction renders the person unable to take the kind of actions that would protect them.

Whether a trauma occurs at home or out in the world, it has a lasting effect on the body and psyche—the body remembers as well as the mind. Various therapies help to heal the body/mind wounds. Sometimes these hidden wounds can lead to destructive repeating of the trauma, called "repetition compulsion."

According to Judith Herman, author of *Trauma and Recovery*, "Traumatized people feel and act as though their nervous systems have been disconnected from the present." This means that the effects of the trauma follow the person throughout life, causing problems such as a strong startle reaction, sensitivity to loud noises, fears, phobias, nightmares, and depression.

During the last few years, a great deal of research has been done on the physiology and chemistry of the brain in relation to trauma and emotion. One new discovery is that traumatic memories are stored differently from regular memories, which makes them harder to resolve. For instance, people who have been traumatized may have recurring dreams or tell or write a story repetitively, as if a phonograph needle is stuck in the groove of the trauma.

It is possible for you to heal trauma and live a fuller, more expressive, and freer life. Writing your stories is an opportunity to put the old ghosts to rest. If need be, you can approach certain memories and issues indirectly rather than confront them head on. Pennebaker told his subjects that if a topic was too painful, they should write about something else.

Take care of yourself. Be your own best friend. There is so much to write about without taking on everything right away. If you do decide to write about what's hidden in the closet, you can alternate between the dark and the light stories as a way of protecting your psyche from becoming overwhelmed.

Writing the Dark and Light Stories

The critic within us and the critics outside us keep us silent. However, old wounds have a way of reasserting themselves into our current lives. The path of self-growth is a path of self-development and transcendence. Writing can be a powerful tool in this process, but it is important to keep ourselves safe and balanced as we unearth our stories.

We all want to avoid unnecessary pain, and our defense system helps us to avoid it. Yet healing comes from balancing our system, and not staying trapped by situations, memories, or feelings that limit our options for living full lives. Our fears, worries, bad dreams, anger, jealousy, insecurity, and pain are real. These feelings can at times get in the way of living a more positive life characterized by a sense of peace, forgiveness of self and others, and renewed energy.

So it is important to write the difficult stories, but consider weaving back and forth between your dark and light memories to prevent yourself from being re-traumatized.

Start with one of the dark qualities in the list below.

The darker topics

Pain	Rejection
Loss	Despair
Vulnerability	Depression
Fear	Jealousy
Longing	Death
Abuse	Illness

• Freewrite about one of the topics for 15-30 minutes.
• Do your feelings, thoughts, and reflections shift after writing? Journal about what you observe.

Next, choose a memory that evoked one of the following positive qualities and write that story.

Qualities of light

Peace	Love
Vulnerability	Trust
Joy	Awe
Generosity	Selflessness
Serenity	Courage

Think about your writing and reactions:

• What happened during the writing, and afterward?

• Try to write a dark story to see if it can shift into a lighter story.

• Write a story where the beginning is darkness and the end is light, or the reverse.

• Balance your memoir writing sessions between dark and light stories to keep yourself in emotional balance.

The path of emotional healing is often like cleaning out an old wound: it hurts while we are cleaning it out, but we feel so much better afterward. It helps to have an ongoing practice that keeps the healing progressing. Here are some suggestions for your regular writing sessions.

• Make a list of the darker memories that trouble you from time to time.

• Write down the age you were when these difficult times happened.

• Write down what you did to cope with the event at the time.

• How do you feel now about the incident?

• What would you have liked to happen differently?

Be sure to honor yourself in the process. Because the goal of this writing is healing, give yourself permission to listen to the stories that your mind and hand lead you to. If you find that you can't stop writing the same story, you might need therapy or some other kind of structured emotional support.

Choosing to revisit different vignettes and times in your life cycle offers different points of view. As you write about yourself at different ages and in new voices, you will be writing and witnessing from multiple perspectives, weaving a larger, more integrated story of your life. (See the developmental questionnaire on page 244 to find other stages that are important for you to write about.)

A trauma is resolved if you are no longer troubled by it and your life is relatively free of a negative reaction to the event. Resolution means that your life is not circumscribed by your fears and you're not disturbed when you remember the traumatic event. In other words, the traumatic event is remembered, but without the degree of emotional reaction that you felt before. It is simply an event that happened, part of the story of your life.

Writing Invitations

1. Protect the vulnerable person in you by distancing in the writing. First, write about what happened in the third person: "she" or "he" instead of "I." Write as if you are watching the event in a movie.

2. Write a scene about a difficult incident, but make it turn out the way you would have wanted it to. Change the incident so it ends more pleasantly and positively.

3. Tell what happened before and after a difficult incident. Write around it, but not about the event itself.

4. Make a bare-bones list of what happened and put it aside. Notice your feelings as you make the list.

5. Make a list of the dark topics or stories that you know are there, but you aren't ready to write yet. List them by title or theme.

6. Make a list of the light stories, stories that bring you a feeling of well being, happiness, contentment, and safety. They may include memories about love, spiritual experiences, and miracles.

7. When you are ready, choose from the "light" list to write a story.

8. When you feel ready, write one of the dark stories.

9. Alternate as needed to write your memoir in a way that feels balanced and safe.

5

 Discovering, Facing, and Writing the Truth

When we let our own light shine, we unconsciously give other people permission to do the same. As we are liberated from our own fear, our presence automatically liberates others.

—Marianne Williamson

"Truth" is a tricky subject these days, especially after the James Frey incident in early 2006, when truth and lie in memoir writing was in the national news and on Oprah. After deciding where to begin, the biggest challenges for writing a memoir, according to the people I have worked with over the years, are issues about writing the truth, telling the truth, facing the truth.

What is truth? Who defines it? How do you understand it? When we choose to write memoir, we are diving into the rivers of memory to come up with our own version of what happened. We are going to investigate the memoirist's journey through landscapes that are often fraught with stumbling blocks for the completion of our memoirs.

Writing a memoir invites us to reflect and explore who we are and who we were at a deeper level than ever before. As we begin to write our stories, we realize that our point of view, our "truth," is often different from that of our families. We discover there are levels of truth, and that some of them have been hidden in our unconscious, only to stream out of the end of the pen.

Did you grow up with these behavioral rules?

- Always tell the truth.
- Don't tell lies.
- Honesty is the best policy.
- You will be punished if you lie.

Are these phrases familiar?

- Don't air the family laundry.
- Family business stays behind closed doors.
- Quit blabbing about your personal business.
- Stop that navel gazing.
- You have quite an imagination!

Many writers and other creative people have been the truth tellers/shit disturbers in their families. They were the different ones, the loudmouths, the ones who challenged the family rules and myths. Such people often grow up to have strong voices, ideas, opinions of their own.

In a very "close" family, one that is threatened by differences, dissenting voices must be brought into line. Thinking differently, having one's own version of the truth, is perceived as dangerous to the established power structure.

There is a force in families called homeostasis that serves to keep everyone together. In such families, you must obey the rules. If you break the rules, you are threatening to everyone else. You must conform or become the scapegoat of the family. As a result, you may feel that you aren't accepted or valued for who you are.

This is excellent, though painful, training for becoming an artist or writer. However, it can also mean enduring the painful exclusion from the kind of acceptance you might yearn for. You may find yourself feeling the outsider in ways that are hard to bear.

Truthtellers Out in the Cold

Humans are social beings, and we need the company of others, even though as writers we are capable of spending long hours alone, at our desks or simply dreaming, thinking, creating.

As beginning writers, we often stop before we get started, hearing familiar critical voices in our heads, warning us not to speak the truth. If you have been shamed, threatened, or shunned by your family for telling the truth, chances are you have a very strong inner critic that fights with your creative force and gets in the way of your full expression.

The inner critic strives to enforce the old rules—stopping us from writing down what we really think or having us pull back from the "real" truth. Over time, we become familiar with this negative inner voice, as with a difficult friend.

But if you are to write your truth, you need to trade in your destructive inner voices for positive ones and find an antidote to the negative programs of old. This may mean more autonomy from the family, or at least from the old version of family you carry in your mind, and a new relationship with yourself.

I have had experiences with facing the truth that taught me a lot, and eventually helped me write my truth despite my inner critic, which was always loud and destructive. When I have faced the challenge of writing the truth, a niggling voice has often piped up: Just change it a little to save face. Don't tell "that much" truth. What will people think? The inner critic begins harassing me, and sometimes I turn away from the piece at first. But then, as I face the truth head on, digging into the groove of the story, I discover that the writing itself takes me to places I had not planned but needed to go, as if it has its own wisdom.

Years ago, I wrote a short memoir piece called *Who Am I?* I was tempted to change the story to be less revealing, to reduce my self-exposure. The story embarrassed me to some degree, and the level of truth that came out as I wrote didn't seem entirely my idea—some part of me was determined to write revealing truths, and I went along with it. In the end it was exciting, like a pioneer exploring new territory, wondering where the trail will lead. The story went on to win first prize in a contest, which meant that even more people read it! My inner critic went nuts for a few minutes, and then I felt another level of healing. Not only did I speak the truth and write it, I was also rewarded by having others feel it was meaningful and powerful.

Another time, I was challenged by truths I was afraid to know about. I didn't want to know what that small voice murmuring in my left ear had to tell me. I'd noticed it for several months, the sense that there was something dark waiting inside that I needed to discover about me, something in the past. I tried to prepare myself, meditating to be ready for whatever might come forth.

Finally, through several traumatic circumstances in my life, I was forced to face the knowledge that I'd grown up with a grandmother who'd had psychotic episodes. I had known that much of my time with her was dark and frightening, but putting that name to it was terrifying. What did it mean about me? Was I doomed to be crazy too?

I was stricken with both despair and relief. Because I'd faced one of my worst fears, I became less afraid, stronger, and more able to continue healing. The voice in my left ear stopped. I integrated the insight and eventually realized I was not my grandmother, I was not doomed to her fate. It took many years to trust this, and to develop more strength and fewer fears.

Harry Potter's Technique

My writing students tell me they are afraid the past will overwhelm them when they start writing. Writers soon become aware that what they intend to write is not always what emerges. Sometimes our writing takes us past the barred gates and unwelcome memories come rushing out. How can we cope with this new knowledge? How can we face our truths, no matter how unwanted?

Recently, as I watched a Harry Potter movie, I took note of a technique that helped Harry confront terror. He was coached to hold in his mind the best memory of his life while he cast a spell on a terrifying apparition that represented his deepest fears. If the positive image was not strong enough, the spell would not work.

I have suggested a similar technique to my students, though we have had to make do without a magic wand. I talk with them about light and dark stories. "Light" stories bring light and healing, happiness and hope, love and forgiveness; dark stories are about wounds that are still unhealed, pain, loss, grief, and fear.

Jung talks about the repressed shadow in the human psyche, the parts of us we don't want to know about. However, when we face the shadow side of ourselves, we become more integrated and free to be whole.

One thing is certain: facing our truths, whether major upheavals in our lives or smaller day-to-day events, helps us to grow. Each time we face ourselves, who we are and who we have been, we build strength for the present and the future.

Start gently. Begin with your light stories and gradually call forth the dark ones. Tell the stories of your life in a safe way that inspires you to move forward, in your writing and your healing.

Writing Invitations

1. Write a story your family would call "false," a lie, not true.

2. Write a story your family would call true, but you think is false.

3. Write a scene about your family that speaks of its philosophical truth about life, such as "we are very close," "we are not religious," "we are not prejudiced," etc.

4. What stories would your family tell about you that you feel did not happen?

5. Do you have stories in your mind, or memories, where you doubt the veracity or the accuracy of the memory? Write about it.

6. What family secret(s) do you feel you are obliged to keep? Make a list.

7. How do you feel about secrets as a memoir writer? Journal about this.

8. Write a story you promised never to write.

The Process of Healing

Reading and weeping opens the door to one's heart, but writing and weeping opens the window to one's soul.

— M. K. Simmons

All my life, I have been interested in how people can heal. For the last twenty-seven years I have had a private therapy practice, and have been blessed to work with wonderful clients. I respect and learn from them. As we work together, I hear about their families and how they all came to be who they are.

My clients arrive with a variety of woes, most commonly depression. Their childhoods may have included extreme dysfunctional behavior—alcoholism, abandonment, and emotional abuse. However, they appear normal, functioning well, with jobs, families, and normal activities. Their wounds are hidden and secret. As the work deepens, their masks are gradually stripped away, revealing tremendous secret pain.

A therapy office is a sacred space. In a sacred space, there is safety, trust, openness, vulnerability, and truth. I urge my clients to speak their deepest truths to me, especially those truths that have been too painful to think about. The therapeutic space becomes a place to lay down old burdens and open up new vistas of self-development, but sometimes clients are unaware of their repressed pain.

Loosening the Grip of the Past

When an event occurs that is too upsetting for us to absorb and understand, automatic reactions called defenses take over to protect us from psychic pain. We learn from our families how to deal with painful realities. Family defense patterns, habits and differing points of view are passed on from generation to generation, creating a web of confusion about what the "truth" is. These patterns help to maintain the family's often erroneous or distorted view of itself, which is called the family myth.

It is my job as therapist to gently and gradually penetrate a client's web of beliefs and myths, which often cover up a deeper, more painful story. By asking lots of nosy questions, I find out what really went on behind the closed doors of the childhood home.

For some people, the difficult issues at home are easy to pinpoint. In a house with slammed doors, raised voices, and broken dishes, the problem is obvious. But in some families, the volume is turned down, and there is an elaborate dance to protect the feelings of the parents. In a normal-looking home, it is more difficult to identify problems because they are underground and invisible.

While I work to uncover new levels of truth on the path to healing, I stress to the client that the purpose is not to cast blame but to bring to light hidden wounds carried since childhood. I assume that parents have done their best. However, the client needs to come to terms with the whole truth of the family situation. Without discovering the real circumstances of childhood, it is impossible to resolve the pain it caused and continues to cause.

In the final analysis, it is not a confrontation with parents that leads to resolution of old issues, but a confrontation with one's self. The therapeutic and healing goal is to free ourselves of the aspects of the past that hold us back and to release patterns that keep us from being all of who we are, our best selves.

So when you write about the years of your childhood, you

will explore ever deepening layers of feelings and perceptions about yourself and your family. You will uncover forgotten layers of memory, and you may find yourself questioning your life-long assumptions.

Writing about your childhood can help you know:

- Who you are
- How you think and feel
- What your life story is about
- The meaning and direction of your life
- How to heal

If the idea of writing about the effects of your traumatic emotional or physical experiences worries you, stop and ask yourself:

- How am I feeling right now?
- Am I in my body, feeling my feelings?
- Do I feel safe and comfortable?
- Would writing help me to release stress?

If your answers to those questions are in the negative, then engage in nurturing activities that will comfort and renew you. It is important to "contain" emotional expression of painful memories when you are feeling vulnerable. Practice containment by becoming involved in a positive activity that keeps you away from deep feelings for a while.

On the other hand, if you think that writing would be comforting and would help you to reduce stress, set a timer for five minutes and write. Or alternate short bursts of writing with another pleasant activity to balance things out.

Self-nurturing

Nurturing, comfort, and emotional soothing are necessary to the human organism, but sometimes they are missing in situations of abuse or trauma. Children who grow up in abusive environments learn that they must rely only on themselves. Independence can be healthy, but if it's carried too far, it becomes neglect. An arid wasteland without comfort or connection becomes internalized in the child, and it can be difficult for an adult from this kind of background to receive nurturing or to nurture herself. Lack of self-nurturing can be as seemingly minor as not drinking enough water or as major as self-destructive behavior.

Allowing the self to receive from others is a powerful healing act when we have been taught to keep our needs minimal or non-existent. Trust needs to be established again, with the self as well as with others. If you have been abused, you need to make a transition from internal judgments and that arid wasteland to self-nurturing and an environment in which you can give yourself what you need.

Soothing and nurturing help to repair the tears in the fabric of our childhood. Although different people consider different behaviors to be nurturing, all such behaviors have one thing in common: they bring a sense of peace and well-being.

When I want to relax at the end of the day, my kitties give me some of the nurturing I need. I love stroking their soft fur and hearing them purr. My shoulders relax and I sit back, filled with a sense of peace. Some people are soothed by classical music, a warm bath, well-prepared and tasteful food, or a clean house. Gardening, exercise, and aromatherapy are just a few of the other ways you can create physical and emotional nurturance.

Good Memories as a Nurturing Practice

Writers all know that capturing wonderful, numinous moments from our childhoods makes us feel extra warm and happy, as if we are bringing those special moments into our lives now and filling up the empty places in our hearts.

We remember that child person that we were, how we looked at the world with such amazement and awe and wonder. We think of times that will never exist again, times in history that can never be repeated—an amazing baseball game, the scent of a charcoal fire in the backyard in summer, the wonder of the mountains and trees and a bowlful of stars at night.

Perhaps we remember our teachers and mentors, or the way we

caught fireflies in a jar, the sound of crickets chirping or the hoot of an owl. Our senses have captured many moments that have shaped our psyches into who we have become, and if we are lucky we have many memories that are uplifting or positive that help to balance the hard times we have had.

"There were no good times!"

One student I worked with was writing so many traumatic stories and was so upset by them, that I suggested she write some positive stories to help her balance her writing (and emotional life.) She shouted that she had only one good memory, and there were no good stories. It was all bad. I suggested that she write what she could remember that was good and bring it in the next week.

At the next class, she flew into the room with a smile on her face, waving a sheaf of papers at us. "I found so many more memories that I had forgotten. I really thought there was only one paragraph of good memories, but when I started writing some of the good things, I began to remember more and more of them. Now I realize there were many good times among the bad."

Her story evolved in a new way, one that allowed her more balance, and she found that she had a sense of humor, as well!

Some of my special, numinous moments took place in a summer rose garden in the town where I grew up. The doves who-whoed, the Oklahoma wind blew through my hair, and a breeze warm and sensual wafted the scent of roses toward me as Uncle Maj lifted the head of each flower, inviting me to bury my nose in its petals. I inhaled the sweetness of roses and heard the sounds of airplanes from the nearby air base and the buzzing of cicadas swirling around me.

I inhaled too the sense of safety I felt at Uncle Maj's house, where he lived with his wife, Aunt Helen, my grandmother's best friend. Here there was no yelling, no sharp words, just home-baked bread and the scent of earth and roses. I was protected here, and for the rest of my childhood these people made sure I was safe and gave me all the nurturing they could. Even when they could do nothing in an active way, I could see in their eyes that they were viewing me with a sense of warmth and love.

This memory has lifted me from sorrow many times in my life. I wanted to capture it in words not only to share its beauty and its healing qualities but also to share the love I was given by these two special people. They were "compassionate witnesses," to use Alice Miller's term, and without them, I might not have survived.

Hopefully you have some good memories to feast on in times of trouble, reminding you that you have a safe harbor.

Writing Invitations

1. Make a list of good memories. Select four of them to write as stories.

2. Write about how you have resolved traumatic events in the past.

3. How have memories of their past affected members of your family?

4. List five favorite ways that you nurture yourself. Write about five more for particularly stressful circumstances. Be specific. Describe time, place, and activity.

5. Rank nurturing behaviors in terms of what works best when you are emotionally stressed. Do the same for physical stress.

7. Write about experiences you remember that were healing for you. Write them in the present tense.

7

Witnessing and Self-Nurturing

We are cups, constantly and quietly being filled. The trick is, knowing how to tip ourselves over and let the beautiful stuff out.

—Ray Bradbury

n her books *Drama of the Gifted Child, For Your Own Good,* and *The Truth Will Set You Free,* Alice Miller, a German psychiatrist, writes about the prevalence of child abuse, and how the wounds of child abuse affect people in adulthood. She believes that for victims to heal, the secret, shameful stories of childhood must be revealed and expressed to a compassionate, enlightened witness.

Miller believes that if another person becomes aware of the unfortunate situation we are in, and we are witnessed with compassion by that person, we don't become trapped in the darkness of it. She writes about the helping witnesses many of us were lucky enough to encounter as children—often an aunt, uncle, grandparent, or teacher: "A helping witness is a person who stands by an abused child . . . offering support and acting as a balance against the cruelty otherwise dominant in the child's everyday life."

As adults, telling our stories to a therapist or spiritual teacher helps us to heal. That person becomes an "enlightened witness," someone trained to fully understand the story. The enlightened witness sees us as the whole, beautiful being that we are. Miller says, "Therapists can qualify as enlightened witnesses, as can well-informed and open-minded teachers, lawyers, counselors, and writers."

Witnessing Ourselves through Story Writing

Writing stories and sharing them in a group has been a powerful healing experience for all the students in my groups. People heal at different rates, often through surprising and seemingly ordinary happenings, but story writing often works quickly by turning us into our own compassionate witnesses as the story unfolds.

This witness is the narrator "I" as it tells the story of the "character," a younger version of who we are now. The narrator "I" comments and connects the elements of your story, while also being the main character in it. This dual consciousness is integrative and healing, and unique to memoir writing.

Often we feel we need forgiveness for what happened to us as children. Even as adults, many of us feel that we deserved the abuse we received, or that decisions others made were our own fault. Unfortunately, children take on the responsibility of the adults when they don't understand what is happening to them. They think that the anger of the adults is their fault, or that the reason their parents got a divorce is their fault because they were bad.

Your memoir may have different sections and separate narrative lines that together tell the whole story. The narrative line is the invisible thread that weaves through your story, connecting its themes and sections.

Your book might contain:

• The story of your adult life and how it was shaped by childhood.
• Your childhood story, which could exist in separate chapters.
• An adult voice, looking back with wisdom on the events of childhood and the influence they had on your development.

When you write your life story, you are at once a witness to it and its narrator and author. When you write the true story of your life, you witness what happened, and take a position about your thoughts and feelings as you put the past in perspective.

Story as Witness

Pennebaker's studies complement what Alice Miller has been saying for years—that emotional wounds are carried in the body and need to be released through talking, writing, and expressing emotions. This release helps us integrate our experiences and frees us from self-destructive repetitive cycles.

How to shape the story of your life, and how much to put on paper about other family members should you decide to publish your memoir, are discussed later in this book. Your first focus should be on the memories you need to write about for your own healing, stories that witness your feelings and experiences and explore how you were molded into who you are, with all your strengths and weaknesses.

We are a part of all that has happened to us, and it is all a part of us. Our task as memoir writers is to come to terms with the negative experiences in our lives and balance them with the life-enhancing, happy, and joyous events that were also a part of our pasts.

Many Voices, Many Witnesses

There are various ways to witness ourselves and the stories of our lives. All kinds of artistic self-expression are powerful methods, including painting, gardening, and writing poetry. I learned another method of witnessing and being witnessed through Speaking Circles®, a program created by Lee Glickstein. In his book *Be Heard Now*, Glickstein talks about how the support of a positive group of people changes lives and provides a healing environment.

"When people give us complete positive attention, we can let ourselves feel the old fears and know that nobody will criticize, interrupt, or psychoanalyze us. No one will take over the conversation. No one will imply that there's something wrong with anyone. We are honored for whatever we say, or don't say. It's our time and our space in which to be completely appreciated. That is the healing."

In this creative and alive listening environment, the deeper self is heard and received by the group. The stories are "listened out" of each group member in an environment of complete acceptance and unconditional positive regard. I found this to be a powerful and inspiring experience that helped me with my writing.

When we have not been received in this way, we feel inadequate and empty. We feel that there isn't enough of ourselves to support our own healing work, and this causes despair. We need to learn how to listen to ourselves as we are listened to by a good friend, a therapist, a minister. As writers, we need to learn how to receive ourselves fully and unconditionally within our own skins.

Doreen Hamilton, director of training for Speaking Circles International and a colleague of Lee Glickstein and mine, offers programs that teach people how to create a positive listening environment and move into transformation.

If you have been abused or if memories haunt you, consider therapy along with writing about your past. If you become upset or overwhelmed, be sure to seek the support of friends and colleagues, as well as professional helpers. They hold the position of enlightened witness and compassionate listener. We may need that objective person to "listen the story out of us", to help us understand and reframe what we believe and how we hold our memories.

Hopefully you were blessed to have compassionate witnesses during your childhood who really saw you and noticed who you were, even if they could do little actively to help. For some children that witness was a pet, often their only friend. As an adult, you can cultivate compassionate witnesses among your friends, relatives, and colleagues, or you can choose to work with professionals who play that role.

Sometimes, a sense of being witnessed, accepted, and embraced can come from quite an unexpected source, as the following story suggests.

An Accidental Witness

I am a part of all I have met.
—Alfred Lord Tennyson

I still remember the moment when I first heard that line by Tennyson. I was sitting in my high school journalism class listening to Miss Scott philosophize. She sat at the big wooden desk in the front of the room. She wore cotton dresses over a generous yet contained figure, and she had Betty Davis eyes that seemed to see everything. Officially, she taught journalism, but I remember being inspired by all that she brought to the classroom.

At that time in my life, I was barely making it. A good friend had recently committed suicide, and my grandmother had changed from a kind caretaker into a screaming monster. I realized that the only way to survive was to get out of high school and out of town, but I often wondered if I would be able to escape. My despair came from watching the grandmother who had once rescued me, the grandmother who used to call me Sugar Pie and stroke my hair, turn into someone I didn't recognize. I had many secrets because one didn't "air the family's dirty laundry."

That spring afternoon in journalism class, the windows were open and the air smelled sweet and hopeful. I looked out at the fresh greening trees and the blue sky. Then I heard Miss Scott: "I am a part of all I have met."

The world stopped. I raised my hand and asked Miss Scott to repeat what she had said. She spoke the phrase again, and as she did, something shifted inside me. The usual tight knot in my stomach loosened and a sense of well-being came over me. Everything that had happened in my life—my mother's leaving me, my grandmother's going crazy, my friend dying—all of it knitted together into a fabric of meaning. Everything that had been painful and confusing was simply a part of my life. I could receive it in a new way. I was a part of everything, and it all was a part of me.

I realized that day that literature was about the exploration of the deep truths that underlie everyday reality. Miss Scott did not know what was wrong in my life, but it seemed as if she had witnessed me. Or was it Tennyson? My teacher, and literature, gave me something to hold onto.

Writing Invitations

1. Write about a witness who saw the real you when you were a child. Who was this person or animal? What was your relationship with him or her?

2. How did you know this person saw you? How did you feel about being witnessed?

3. Think about a compassionate witness who observed you well, who seemed to see and understand you. Tell the story of how you first met this person, how you felt about him or her, and when you realized that this person was paying special attention to you or witnessing you.

4. Write stories about your witnesses. What positive aspects exist in your life thanks to those who witnessed you?

5. Select two nurturing and fun activities that you plan to do in the next two weeks.

6. Write about childhood nurturing you received, from people, pets, food, games, books, etc.

7. What activities made you feel comforted and secure when you were a child? What smells, sounds, and sights were soothing and nourishing?

8. How do you define listening?

9. How do you know you are being listened to? What people have listened well to you in your life?

Writing with a Beginner's Mind

The voyage of discovery lies not in finding new landscapes but in having new eyes.

—Marcel Proust

I n his book *Zen Mind, Beginner's Mind*, Shunryu Suzuki writes about freeing the mind through meditation, creating the possibility of a fresh and truly open mind, especially when approaching new things. He says that we should look at everything with curiosity and acceptance, and be both vulnerable enough and strong enough to not know everything, to withstand discomfort, to be humble.

When you write with a beginner's mind, you see your story through new eyes. When you write your story the way you see it, not the way it has always been told, you free yourself from the strictures of a "right" way to view the world. If your story doesn't agree with the point of view of other family members, you may feel lonely or even crazy. But still, this is what you know, this is your truth.

Using beginner's mind gives us permission to write what we don't know and to write what has never been written before.

Writing and meditation have much in common: inner listening, quiet and isolation, openness. Sometimes we resist writing just as we resist being alone with ourselves. We stay busy and don't take time to escape from the demands of a noisy, outward-directed life. The Buddhists call a mind filled with these mental distractions a "monkey mind." Like a monkey, it chatters away, distracting us from our true self, a deeper part of ourselves that might be called spiritual.

Meditation is about awareness without attachment to a particular idea or thought. When we meditate, our thoughts are allowed to pass across the mind like clouds. When we write, critical thoughts can get in the way as we judge and critique our writing, and ourselves. Part of our healing practice is to accept our inner creative voices, to hear the deeper truth of who we are. We need to write with openness.

Meditation to Relax

To encourage our inner listening process, it helps to put aside the stresses of regular life and relax. We need to let go of our busy thoughts as we make room for other voices, feelings, and parts of ourselves.

To help access our inner listening, we can learn to relax and focus on our breath. Breathing well and deeply is the basis for all letting go of stress. When we focus on our breath and our relaxed muscles, we can feel ourselves getting pleasantly heavier and warmer. When we relax the tension in our muscles, a tense mind lets go as well, promoting the flow of creativity.

When you're ready to do this relaxation meditation, find a comfortable place to sit or lie down. Set a timer for twenty or thirty minutes. After you learn how to relax, you can obtain the same benefit in less time.

Settle in a comfortable place and take some deep breaths. Feel yourself becoming present and aware of your body. This will enhance listening to your inner voice, the positive one, the one that nurtures you, the one that supports all your efforts to write and to speak.

Bring to mind an image of a living being that makes you happy. Some people think of a loved one—a mother, father, aunt, uncle, friend, or favorite pet. Feel the feelings you have when you are being hugged or touched lovingly by this person or being. As you think of this, imagine golden light flowing down from the top of your head into your shoulders, and let it spill down your body, breathing deeply without forcing, just gentle breaths. Allow yourself to feel the warmth that this visualization brings, filling your body with well-being.

Feel the warmth in your wrists and hands, your fingers, your arms. Let your muscles relax, the muscles of your body and mind that sometimes keep you tight. Ask them to allow you to write, to express yourself. Think of being encouraged by your pet or favorite person. Have fun with this; don't be too serious. Imagine being gently massaged or comforted. Breathe these feelings into your body. If you have a favorite, safe place, either in real life or in your imagination, bring it to mind now.

When you are relaxed, when the mind and body are in harmony and your thoughts are flowing freely like a stream, rest in the peace of this state for a few minutes, then write for five minutes or longer.

Meditation to Your Past Self

Now you will be guided into remembering earlier parts of your life. Follow the exercise as far as you like. If you become uncomfortable, stop and return to the present.

See yourself at the age you are now. Picture how you look, what you are wearing, the shape of your life. See yourself in your mind's eye: your body, your clothes in your favorite colors, your hair, face, and skin. See the people you spend time with, the things you are most proud of.

Now imagine the calendar flying back to ten years ago. What did you look like then? What style of clothes were you wearing? Where were your favorite restaurants or clubs? What did you do in your leisure time? See if you can remember who you spent time with and what you did. What were your hopes and dreams?

Go back another ten years and ask yourself these same questions. Decade by decade, revisit who you were, what you were doing, what you were feeling, wanting, and dreaming.

Notice—but don't dwell on—any issues and problems that you faced during each decade. What were you trying to heal or avoid? How did that work for you? Think about your hopes and dreams. What was the best part about your life? How did you feel about yourself during each period of your life? What was your favorite color, food, vacation? Who were your friends, pets? What books influenced your life?

See yourself all the way back into your adolescence and then into childhood. See your body, feel how it felt to be twenty, fifteen, ten, five. See yourself in your clothes, inside your room, in your house. Who were the people in your family back then? What did they look like, sound like? Notice the memories that have formed you and are a part of you.

Now pick up your pen and write about one of the scenes you just pictured. Write a vignette; sketch out what you remember without anchoring it to a story. This memory exercise can help you bring the past into focus and help you picture important scenes in your life that may have receded into your unconscious mind.

For more relaxation and memory meditations, see Appendix A.

Writing Invitations

1. Write about what "beginner's mind" means to you. What new beginnings have you had in your life? List at least ten.

2. Find photos for each decade of your life. Write about these topics for each decade:

   a. What was most important to you during these years?

   b. What was the best part of your life; the worst?

   c. Write about your hopes and dreams.

   d. Describe your favorite clothes, and activities.

   e. What were your mother and father like during this time?

   f. How about brothers, sisters, or other family members?

3. Describe your grandmother; your grandfather.

4. What life lessons did you learn from them?

5. What legacy did they pass on to you?

9

Beyond the Journal: Writing True Stories as a Way to Heal

Two or three things I know for sure, and one of them is that to go on living, I have to tell stories, that stories are the one sure thing I know to touch the heart and change the world.

—Dorothy Allison

*W*riting a memoir is a long process that requires different kinds of writing. The first level is like journaling, where thoughts, images, memories, and associations spill onto the page as quickly as possible, without censoring. A first draft is composed of a stream-of-consciousness flow of imagery without much structure or logical sense.

I tell my students that this chaos is necessary for the healing aspect of the writing. Often when we try to impose a structure prematurely, we are covering up painful stories or trying to keep in control the outflow of memories that frighten us or worry us, as if their escape is dangerous to us. If we learned in the past that telling the truth and openly sharing the family secrets is dangerous to our well-being, this caution has been deeply learned. We need to unlearn it in order to craft our memoirs.

When we write memoir, the part of us that wants to heal demands to be heard. It demands that the unbidden stories erupt onto the page. Some of my students are afraid of this process, but when they come to understand that it is a necessary, though emotionally challenging, part of the writing, they are able to let the deep stories emerge.

I make my students promise not to compare their first drafts with published works or with other writers. We often subject our fragile first drafts to a terrible scrutiny, which is premature, unfair, and activates the inner critic. Allow your journaling to continue and your raw narrative to spill out. Eventually, another layer emerges—the drive to develop and craft it as a story.

What is a story?

Pennebaker called a narrative, a story, "A type of knowledge." I found this comment quite fascinating and began to explore the ways in which a story is a kind of knowledge. Teaching and coaching have taught me how this is so. My students' stories contain several layers: the factual—what happened, when, where, etc.—and a "wisdom layer, the insightful voice that evolves over time as we write.

I have already touched on this split consciousness between the narrator and the character of the story. It is a powerfully healing aspect of memoir writing, but it can be confusing. It helps to think of the observer as a camera lens that captures the unfolding story, while the character inhabits the body of the "I" that the story is about.

Here is one popular definition of story: a narrative with a beginning, a middle, and an end.

While this seems self-evident, what it means is that we "construct" a story, creating a way for the telling of events to evolve into a climax and a resolution. The creation of a story goes beyond journaling to the idea of using fictional tools, such as scenes, that allow the story to be "shown" rather than "told."

A healing memoir requires the use of scenes as a way to bring you, the writer/narrator, back to the time you are remembering. As writers, we again become the six-year-old whose father dies or the little girl who misses her mother. When we bring ourselves into intimate contact with who we once were and at the same time witness ourselves, our perspective is transformed, giving us more freedom to be who we really are.

One reason story writing is so important is that it does more than give structure and meaning to an event; it provides a way to heal emotionally. After writing their memoirs, many people report that they are no longer haunted by disturbing memories and the emotions they evoke. The writing process has helped them integrate their life experiences and resolve old issues.

Writing Scenes Using Sensual Details

Most people, having gone to schools and taken the required English classes, have learned how to write essays, and how to construct a narrative that compresses and summarizes. We were taught that good writing leaves out all unnecessary detail.

But writing stories is different. Here is an example of a narrative that does *not* use sensual details or scenes. I think you'll agree it is not very gripping.

When I grew up in Columbia in the state of Missouri, I was born to parents Ben and Sally. I had five brothers and sisters and we got along well except when my older brother beat me up. I enjoyed playing baseball and family holiday gatherings. I got good grades in school, which pleased my mother.

We live in a world full of sensual experience. When we write, we need to allow ourselves to feel this sensual world and bring it to the page. Writing our sensations means choosing words and associations that stimulate sight, sound, taste, smell, and touch in the mind of the reader.

Sight Use color, shape, texture, and other specific details to describe how things look. Specificity helps us remember better.

Sound Many memories are associated with intense sounds, such as loud noises—screaming, storms—anything that overwhelms our senses. Even small sounds—a clock ticking, keys jingling, a cat mewing—may evoke potent memories. Most powerful of all may be the sound of silence. Of course, some sounds evoke happy memories—the ticking of a grandfather clock, a rushing stream, the ocean, and music.

Taste Our taste buds are particularly sensitive during childhood. Some of our best memories involve food and spice: the first time we ate a particular food, or our favorite meal or dessert.

Smell Our olfactory sense may be the most powerful of all. Memory is easily evoked through experiencing a smell or scent connected with a particular person or event—the smell of someone's perfume; the way a particular person's clothes smell like no one else's; the smell of lilacs, oranges, or the sea.

Touch Our skin can apparently retain the memory of a particular feeling, for example, the texture of rough or smooth surfaces, such as leather, sand, or a cat's fur. Our bodies remember how we felt when we saw our first sunset or when something significant happened—a thrill coursing through the blood or a hollow ache.

Drawing from the summary paragraph at the beginning of this section, below are examples of showing a story in scene and including some sensual detail. Note that the details of the story are *shown* and not just *told*. There would be dialogue and even more sensual detail in a completed piece.

1. **Birth**—*It was a snowy day in December, I've always been told, when I began my arrival into the world. My four brothers and sisters waited impatiently at grandma's house for me to come home with our mother, whom I'd taken away from them. Late in my life they would remind me of this abandonment, but the day I arrived, the photos show their eager faces, from my brother age 10 on down to little Betty, looking at me with wide eyes.*

2. **Place**—*The most memorable thing about living in Columbia as a child was the sudden arrival of amazing thunderstorms. The whole sky would ripple with huge, dark clouds and lighting would flicker across the horizon.*

3. **The conflict with the brother**—*I could tell when Bobby was about to blow. His face would get crinkled, his eyes narrowing like a snake's. His fingers would twitch and I'd try to figure out how to get away.*

4. **Holidays**—*The long table would be loaded with turkey, dressing, two kinds of potatoes, three vegetable dishes, with five pies waiting for us on*

the side table. The jokes would fly around, and no matter what strife there had been, on this day we would celebrate.

5. Good Grades—*Every time I brought home the report card, it was like Christmas. I'd proudly hold out the folded yellow paper printed with the name of the school and mother would nervously wipe her hands on her apron before opening it. Then her expression would change, as if the sun had just come up, her eyes shining. I knew she was proud of me, and I'd do anything to have her look at me like that.*

When you write, allow your mind to capture memories of sensual experiences. Feel, smell, and sense the details that you remember. Keep in mind that the use of sensual descriptions and language creates a feeling in the reader similar to your own experience. This is what you want; you want the reader to feel your world, to enter into your body and mind, and to journey with you into the past through the powers of your imagination and memory.

Stories as Healing

My students discover new information about themselves and their feelings when they take the plunge into writing stories that include clear scenes and sensual detail. One woman wrote about the trauma she experienced at the hands of her mother when she was a small child, a beating that terrified her, but she had forgotten it until a small detail reminded her—a memory of the close-up pattern on a linoleum floor. In the safety of the group, she took herself into the scene completely and into the body of the small child she was when this traumatic event took place.

While it was difficult for her to write the story, reading it was even more challenging. She stood up and read carefully, her hands shaking, about the beating, her feelings, and the decision this beating had caused her to make about herself. She realized that she had remained unconsciously trapped by this event. After she wrote it, she felt released. She felt taller, healthier, and more courageous. Furthermore, the whole class witnessed the suffering of the little girl that she once had been, and she experienced the support and compassion of the group. It was a very healing experience for her to write this traumatic event as a story.

Writing Invitations

1. Describe a memorable morning when you were 4, 9, or 12 years old. Where were you—e.g. country, city, state, building, or open landscape? What were you doing?

2. What was happening around you? Were there adults in your world and what were they doing? How did you feel in your body and in your emotions?

3. Write about a favorite house—your own or someone else's. What was the mood in the house, the smells, and sensual world of the house? What happened there of importance to you?

4. Write about the smells and sounds of your childhood world. A farm world has potent smells, as does a city, a neighborhood.

5. Write in scene in the present tense using the "I" point of view.

The Psychology of Memoir Writing

*Those who cannot remember the past
are condemned to repeat it.*

—George Santayana

10

How the Past Shapes the Present

Time present and time past are all present in time future.
—T.S. Eliot

*W*hile you write your memoir, your family and your childhood come to life on the page. As the narrator, you tell the story of the significant things that shaped you and your life, through your own eyes and from your own point of view. Memoir requires reflection, thought about the "how" and the "why" things happened the way they did, as well as the "who, what, when, and where" of a typical story.

When students read their family stories aloud in my class, they are often surprised by their classmates' reactions: they receive unexpected insights and comments about their families and themselves. The reactions of the class reflect views of family dynamics that are different from those the student holds.

Most of us grow up perceiving our family and childhood as "just the way it is," unaware of the many different ways families live and cope with stressful events and disappointments. We begin our writing from this internalized, naïve, perspective, only to find ourselves surprised by how other people react to our stories. When writing a memoir, it is helpful to learn how the family crucible shapes a child, and how child-rearing practices from past generations affect you.

When students understand how tragedy, trauma, or stressful events alter the family, the critic is silenced, and the writer can confront painful memories with greater insight and compassion. The progress of writing a healing story is aided by this knowledge of family psychology.

"Family" can be defined in many ways, and these definitions seem to be expanding as the world changes and gets smaller through technology. Traditionally, "family" refers to a group of people who have a common ancestor or are related by marriage. The nuclear family includes parents and children; the extended family includes a collection of grandparents, aunts, uncles, and cousins, great aunts and uncles, great-grandparents, and people added to the family through marriage. The extended family may also include intimate friends and life partners who are unmarried.

People who were orphaned or grew up in an atypical family will have a more complex history and perhaps more questions to ask as they consider writing their memoirs. Some experience a persistent heartache that accompanies the early death of a parent, abandonment, divorce, or any early loss. Children can feel abandoned even when they live in the same house with their parents if those adults are so dysfunctional or in such pain themselves that they can't be present for the children. Mental or physical illness creates a situation of abandonment for children because the afflicted parent can't really do what is needed to care for them. It can be difficult to sort out this kind of family history because of struggles with guilt: unacceptable, negative feelings vie with feelings of empathy for the ill person. You may think of yourself as selfish if you feel angry about your own unfulfilled needs when your parent is ill. Nonetheless, it is natural to experience those conflicting feelings.

It is important to remember that not all atypical families are dysfunctional. Each family is unique, with strengths that balance some of the more negative traits. In some families, it is difficult to see these points of light, at least early in the healing process, because of the emotional pain that gets in the way of finding compassion. This is why it is important to help your authentic voice to speak and to tell the dark stories that will help you go to the next stage of healing.

For me, growing up with a grandmother and living far away from my divorced parents, I always felt that I was odd, different, and of a lower status than other people. But my grandmother acted as if she was better than everyone, so there was no way to talk about how I felt. I hated filling out those forms where we had to write our mother's and father's names. I had to fill in "guardian" and then endure the questioning looks I thought that word implied: "What happened, what's wrong with your family, why aren't you normal?"

My mother and grandmother often acted bizarrely—screaming, throwing dishes, rushing dramatically to and from trains, and crying during each visit. During my early years, I didn't realize that my grandmother had left my mother when she was young. I could see their pain, but I just wanted us to be like everyone else. (Of course that's a common childhood wish that rarely comes true.) It wasn't until my mother was on her deathbed that I received an official diagnosis for her and my grandmother: manic-depression. Finally, I had a name and an explanation for behaviors that had caused pain for so many people in our family for generations.

Whether we like it or not, family is the training ground for our adult lives, where we discover who we are and who we are not, and where we form the habits and beliefs that we carry with us into adulthood. Theories abound about whether this early learning process is primarily emotional, cognitive, spiritual, or some combination of these.

In 1975, I was drawn to the Fischer-Hoffman Process, my first therapy experience, because of its philosophy: that we are all whole human beings, with physical, mental, emotional, and spiritual aspects. According to Bob Hoffman, founder of the Quadrinity Process and author of *Getting Divorced from Mom and Dad*, we strive to become like our parents, adopting their positive and negative traits to try to please them and gain their unconditional love. We focus on the outside, on getting that love, which can leave us vulnerable and unable to learn how to love ourselves. The therapy experience taught me that in order to find myself, first I had to confront all the repressed "bad" feelings I'd carried through the years, trying to be "good" and likeable. Only then would I be able to see the past clearly and to understand who I am, and who my parents and grandmother were. The idea that, deep down, we are loveable, perfect beings gave me the freedom to search for peace and healing through the years, and provided me with a way to break the pattern that had passed through the generations of my family—three generations of mothers who had emotionally and physically abandoned their daughters.

One of the most significant tools used in this therapy was writing. We wrote for hundreds of hours. During the three months I was involved in the Fischer-Hoffman Process, I wrote autobiographical material for the first time—a negative, emotional version that tore the veils from my eyes.

Writing helps us to see family patterns and dynamics more clearly, and helps us to create a transformed view of ourselves, our identity, and how we feel about our family. Through this refashioned view we can heal old wounds and find the freedom to be ourselves, be more of who we truly are, at a deep and satisfying level.

Writing Invitations

1. Write about the history of connections, abandonment, and losses in your family.

2. Were there behaviors in your family that you did not understand? Make a list of them, and then freewrite some scenes that come to mind.

3. How did you feel during family conflicts? In your body? In your mind?

4. What behaviors and beliefs did you learn from your family?

5. What generational patterns in your family concern you?

6. What positive traits have you adopted from your family?

7. What negative traits do you have that you'd like to change?

11

The Secret Dynamics of Families

Happy families are all alike; every unhappy family is unhappy in its own way.

—Leo Tolstoy

amily stories have a combination of grief, joy, love, hate, and loss. When the writing touches on abuse, alcoholism, rigid religious or political beliefs, separation, or injustice, the writer worries about the family's reactions, and these worries can get in the way of writing. I have observed that if writers gain a greater understanding of family dynamics, it helps them resolve some of their writing conflicts.

Family Dynamics

Family dynamics are a potent and powerful force. They bind the family together in its need to protect itself and stay safe as a unit. Memoir writing goes to the heart of a family's vulnerability. Love and concern for the feelings of others, positive or negative, can silence a writer's voice. Remember that the goal of memoir writing is not to blame parents or anyone else for how you feel and what you think. We all know how powerful family alliances and a family's unwritten rules can be. Even as adults we feel a powerful pull, like the moon tugging the earth, to be silent, to put on a happy face, and to brush aside our need to tell our stories.

It's important to remember these facts about families:
- Each member is doing the best he or she can.
- Most people do not intend to hurt anyone.
- Each person in the family is trying to get needs met, to survive, and to grow into his or her unique birthright: to be a full human being.
- Every person sees the family, his or her place in it, and the roles of other family members from a different perspective.

One important aspect of family dynamics is the jockeying for power and control. Who is the boss? Who makes the important decisions? Normally, in a nuclear family, the parents are at the top of the hierarchy, and they maintain boundaries to protect the marital relationship and the whole family. The children, although governed by the parents, have their own subsystem and sibling dynamics. When the parent and child systems are balanced, the family functions well, with everyone's needs taken care of. When the systems are out of balance, symptoms may develop, such as school problems, illness, and interpersonal conflicts.

I have mentioned homeostasis before, and defined it as an unconscious dynamic in the family that helps restore balance when it has been disturbed. Changes in the family, such as a move, a child leaving home, and certain developmental milestones, may feel like threats. Techniques such as shame and guilt can be used to keep everyone in line. When a family's defense system is broken, previously hidden pain and truth break out into the open.

Telling your truth and writing your memoir can disturb the family's internal balances. How much to break the rules and how to write anyway are decisions that all memoir writers face. You may want to respect your family's point of view, but it is important to consider your own autonomy and your role in the family.

Understanding how families work and how children develop in the context of family may help you decide what to include in your memoir. The following ideas and concepts are used by family therapists to help the families who come to them for help.

Family Roles

Family members take on roles that can become ingrained as part of the family dynamics. According to Claudia Black, author of *It Can't Happen to Me*, the children in a dysfunctional family develop different personas or roles to handle imbalances in the parental system. The eldest child may become the "little parent," the responsible one who makes sure all the homework is done, the food is on the table, and the other members of the family get to school and work. The placater, also called the peacemaker, tries to stop conflict from erupting, calms things down after a fight, and convinces people to kiss and make up. The scapegoat, the black sheep of the family, gets in trouble to distract the family from what is really wrong. The mascot keeps the family laughing by cracking jokes and clowning.

Family members unconsciously slip into these kinds of roles to maintain homeostasis. Most of us take on different roles for a period of time, but in a dysfunctional family the roles become rigidified. When this happens, it may be difficult to change the pattern or to get away from the powerful family energy system.

There are other roles people in a family might adapt. The martyr, for instance, gives up his own needs to meet the needs of others, sacrificing his own happiness often unnecessarily. The payoff is receiving others' gratitude and having a way to control the behavior of other family members.

Another family role is that of victim, who plays the injured party. Though a legitimate injury may have occurred, the person takes on a role, which helps get her needs met, such as appreciation and acknowledgment of her importance. The passive ruler may appear to be the weakest person in the family, but he wields the strength to control other family members. We've all read novels in which Aunt Sissy stays in bed all the time yet wields considerable power from between the covers.

The hero/rescuer role is one we all identify with in movies and stories. The hero/rescuer takes care of everyone and does everything, only to find that there is no time for her own needs to be met; she may suffer illness or psychological stress by trying too hard to keep everyone happy.

Family Rules

Unwritten rules govern families. They help to preserve the family's functioning. To be accepted and "in", you must obey the rules. If you don't, the family's balance will be disturbed. Some typical family rules include:

- Don't embarrass the family.
- Don't be more successful than we are.
- Don't be happier than your [fill in the blank: mother, father, grandfather].
- Be successful and make us proud, no matter what it costs.
- Don't expose us by telling the truth.
- Keep our secrets.
- Don't rock the boat.

I have observed over the years that many memoir writers confront their families' unconscious rules as they put their stories on the page. This offers them new insights and possibilities for healing themselves and even the family as they process new information that arises through the writing.

Family Myths

Family myths control how the family interacts with its members and with the outside world. These myths are unconsciously held beliefs about the family that help to protect it from harsh realities they want/need to avoid. Some family myths include:

- We are better than other people.
- We are more intelligent.
- We are poor but proud.
- We are perfect.
- We always get along.
- We don't get sick.
- Uncle Jake is our hero; he can do no wrong.

The memoir writer may capture the lie beneath these myths through writing family stories, and the family may react to the deeper truths being revealed if they read your work. As you write, you will come to terms with how you need to approach your family about these stories. It is often best to use the whole first draft as a means to your own healing. You can deal with the family later, when you are clearer about the situations and dynamics you are writing about.

The Real Self

Running like a deep stream within us is our "real self"—the part of us that existed before we were born, the part of us that is balanced and wise and able to love. The real self is both a psychological and a spiritual aspect of ourselves. James Masterson, a psychologist and the author of *The Real Self*, says that the real self gets covered up as we form protective defenses. These defenses protect us from emotional pain that would be too great for us to bear. They include processes such as denial (it didn't happen), projection (it's your fault, not mine), and rationalization (I didn't really want that new job anyway).

Masterson says that when the real self is beleaguered by severe, ongoing psychological stress, another mechanism, the false self, is established to protect the fragile real self from disintegration. The false self denies our true feelings and creates a false front, or persona, that faces the world.

Writing a memoir shifts how you perceive these family and individual dynamics. Healing through writing a memoir invites the other parts of us—our creativity, our vulnerability, and the love in our hearts—to return to our consciousness. As this happens, we come back to our real selves, and we heal.

According to developmental psychologists, character and personality are significantly shaped before the age of five. But there are other ways of looking at development—it is life-long, and it's never too late to shape ourselves into a more whole person. Opportunities for growth and healing appear in all seasons of a person's life. As we pass through each stage of development, we encounter opportunities to evolve new strengths, heal old wounds, enhance our creativity and spirituality, and remake ourselves into the best person we can be.

Layers of Self through our Development

When we write a memoir, we encounter our former selves, the children we once were, the teenager, the young adult. Through the years we may have forgotten these shadowy parts of ourselves; writing brings them back to us as we listen intently to a voice within. A brief review of the early developmental stages will help us to better understand our younger selves and to draw on them later as we write the memoir. A developmental approach allows us to see ourselves as whole beings. After all, our behavior is the result of many forces: psychological, social, biological, and spiritual.

For the first few months of life, an infant is merged with his mother, unaware of his own body and without a separate sense of self. According to Margaret Mahler, author of *The Psychological Birth of the Human Infant,* the infant needs to feel secure enough with his mother or mother figure (caregiver) in order to separate from her in a healthy way. When the mother figure meets the child's needs appropriately, the child proceeds smoothly to the next level of development, but if there is stress or if the developmental stages are disturbed by physical separation or some other trauma, the child will be vulnerable to psychological problems later in life. The earlier the wound, the more vulnerable the child will be. One of the cornerstones of human development is the infant's need for secure attachment to a caregiver. The child goes through several stages of separation and differentiation during which, ideally, the caregiver supports the child's exploration of the world and provides unconditional love.

Two-year-olds typically struggle with individuation—the process of becoming individuals in their own right, separate from their primary caregivers. The two-year-old's imperious "No" really means, "This is me; I am not you." Through this stormy period, caregivers need to show the child she is loved, and must provide limits and boundaries with compassion. Two-year-olds may see the world and themselves as all bad or all good; they may be unable to integrate conflicting images and feelings.

By age three, the normally developing child feels secure even when parents come and go. He is now able to integrate conflicting images into a smooth sense of self and others. Physical growth, the acquisition of certain social skills, and cognitive development all help the child understand and interact with his world.

In adolescence the young person repeats certain aspects of earlier developmental stages to integrate them at a new level; this is why teenagers are so passionate about "no" and "yes."

When adolescents leave home, families undergo a major transition. Families show signs of stress and conflict, and must gain balance again in a new form. In dysfunctional families, the necessary adjustments may not be made, leading to further stress and even crisis.

Social Forces that Shape Us

In Chinese, the word for "crisis" and the word for "opportunity" are the same. Family therapists agree that a crisis in the family provides an opportunity for new patterns to develop. Every one of us strives to find balance, love, and acceptance as a unique and wonderful being. Healthy family patterns help us meet those needs.

Events and conditions that create stress in the family, such as the physical or mental illness of a family member, alcoholism, frequent moves, poverty, emigration, and war, may disrupt the developmental timetable and force children to grow up too soon.

Certain developmental patterns may also differ from family to family because of differing ethnic and cultural customs. For example, child-rearing patterns in rural Iowa may differ significantly from those in urban New York. First-generation Chinese-Americans may raise their children differently from third-generation Irish-Americans.

All of the factors that affect child development and the workings of families need to be considered when writing a memoir in order to heal.

Writing Invitations

Let the following questions guide you as you reflect on developmental patterns in your family. Apply the questions to both your own experience growing up in your family and to what you know about the lives of your parents, grandparents, and great-grandparents. You may find generational patterns. Looking at your early years in terms of developmental stages can prevent you from feeling overwhelmed by the many stories you may have to tell. For more developmental questions, see the Appendix.

1. What stories do you know about the early years in the lives of your parents or grandparents? Were they secure, or did they suffer early separation due to illness, moving, immigration, or abandonment?

2. Did your family encourage autonomy and separation, or were children kept at home or taught to cling to parents to meet the adults' needs?

3. How did parents give attention to developing children or show that they were loved and important members of the family?

4. Were children forced to grow up too soon because of family stressors? What were some of these stressors? Write about them first from your point of view and then, if you can, from your mother's and father's points of view.

5. What ethnic and cultural contexts may have affected development in your family?

6. How was punishment used during childhood? What was the manner of discipline, and who delivered it?

7. Were caretakers reliable or did children have to move from family member to family member?

8. Was becoming a "real self" encouraged? How? Show it in a scene.

12

The Genogram

> *I ought to be able to remember the family ties, since my cells are*
> *alive with reminders.*
>
> —Lewis Thomas

The genogram, a map of the family, helps sort out family traits and history. With this map, you can track family characteristics, relationships, and behaviors that are repeated through the generations.

The genogram reveals relationships and repeated family patterns, which can lend insight into your stories. The genogram can be created before you write, or you can write a summary of the story you're going to put in memoir form first and then map the relationships to see the patterns more easily.

Linda's Story Summary and Genogram

The Dickersons and the Stinemans settled in Iowa in the mid-nineteenth century and became farmers in the rich soil near the Mississippi. Of German origin, they were hard workers, strict with children, and proud of their independence. As a young girl, Lulu, who became my grandmother, noticed that the women wore themselves down with housework and too many children. She thought that poverty made for a depressing life, and perhaps she intuitively knew that if she remained a lower class, barefoot farm girl, the fate of these women would be her own.

In 1911, Lulu eloped with Blaine, a middle-class man whose family owned the newspaper in the nearby small town of Wapello. Blaine's father and grandfather were in Iowa politics, and his grandfather was an attorney. I can't imagine his family being very happy about the sixteen year-old farm girl who eloped with their son. Out of this union came a stillborn boy, and then my mother, Josephine Elizabeth, was born.

The marriage suffered from various stresses, and from my grandfather's use of alcohol. All the men in that family drank, and drank to excess. Blaine's youngest sister once told me there never was a gathering in her family when Blaine and his father didn't have a horrible fight—about politics, about which one was right. About anything.

According to Blanche, Lulu left the family when her daughter, my mother, was young. Knowing that my mother had been abandoned too helped me to have empathy for her when she would scream and rage at my grandmother. As the story goes, Josephine lived with various family members, including Blanche's mother, Josephine, for whom she was named. At age twelve or thirteen, she came to Chicago to live with her mother, who had remarried. The battle between mother and daughter began in earnest, and continued until Lulu's death.

When she was twenty-nine, my mother married my father, and I was born nine months later. He lived with us until I was eight months old, and left because of World War II. Later I found out he simply needed to get away from my irrational and hysterical mother.

When I was five, Lulu, whom I called Gram, bought a house for Mother and me to live in with her, which worked out for a few short months, until my mother left, declaring, "I'm going back to Chicago." My stomach flipped and my breath stopped. My body knew without a doubt that this was the end of us as mother and daughter, and I was right.

I stayed with my grandmother, who was rescuing and sweet until she began to dissolve into a rageful and abusive person by the time I was ten. An ongoing family feud, which included my father, finally ended with the death of my grandmother and father during the same week in 1971. When I was twenty, I visited my mother in Chicago, only to find that she didn't want anyone to know she had a daughter. The struggle to get my mother to accept and love me, and then my children, forms the basis of my memoir, ending with a kind of resolution at her deathbed.

The pattern of abandoned daughters and grandmothers—the fights and rejections—seemed destined to go on forever, but I was determined to break it. Through therapy, writing, and learning how to love in new ways, I broke the chain of abandonment. My memoir, *Don't Call Me Mother,* tells this story.

Writing Invitations

1. If you have information about your maternal grandparents, start your genogram with their generation. Draw a long horizontal line to make room for succeeding generations. Use vertical lines to connect your mother and her siblings beneath your grandparents. Do the same for your father's side of the family. On the line connecting husband and wife, write the marriage date and the date of divorce or separation if applicable.

2. Then connect your mother and father with a horizontal line, and use vertical lines to connect to yourself and your siblings.

3. Fill in whatever names and dates you know. If family members have done genealogical research, perhaps you can use their material. But you don't have to do genealogical research to create a genogram.

4. Write a brief summary of your family story. Try to keep it under three pages.

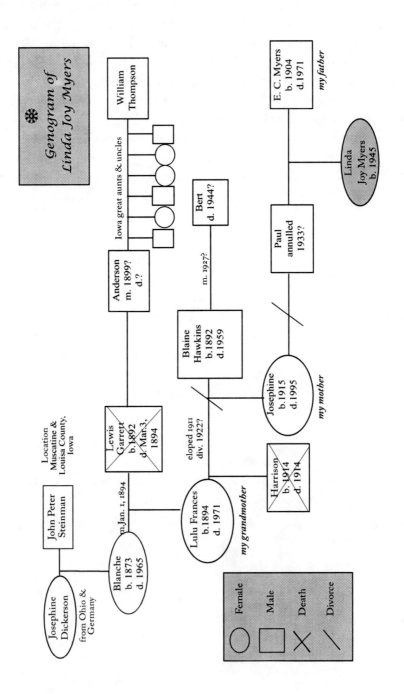

Genogram of Linda Joy Myers

13

Conquering the Inner Critic

*Since we cannot change reality, let us change the eyes
which see reality.*

—Nikos Kazantzakis

 ll of us have one, a voice that starts chattering and criti-
cizing us when we begin to express ourselves. You already
have experienced this inner critic, I'm sure. All writers
I've ever met—in fact all creative people—seem to have it. It tries to
silence us, whispering that we are no good, we should be ashamed
of who we are and what we have to say. Too often we listen to it, and
come to doubt ourselves. We may even put down the pen, believing
its destructive message.

My students talk to me about their inner critic voices, which
range from extremely harsh to seductively soothing. The soothing
voice whispers, "Writing is so hard on you. If you would just stop,
life would be easier. Focus on something else. Besides, if you write
what you really think, your family will hate you."

The critic voice sows seeds of doubt and fear: "You can't say that.
Why do you even try? This is bad, you are bad. This makes no sense.
What will people think?"

Both women and men have this voice, and for those who come

from strict, judgmental, or abusive homes, it may have a particularly sharp edge. If we grow up learning that our needs or thoughts should not be stated, or that it is our responsibility to keep others alive or safe, we learn to denigrate our own voices and selves. We learn how to hide, and keep the shame of the family secret by silencing ourselves.

Most people try to shrug off and ignore the voice, only to find that it gets louder and even more insistent. Some people recognize the voice as that of the family, or of society, shaming them for expressing a differing point of view, or forbidding them to talk about situations that should not be discussed openly. Rather than ignore the inner critic, I suggest paying attention to it so you can learn to release its power over you.

Speaking Up

It is important to name and to write about the inner critic's pronouncements because this destructive force cannot live in the open, only in the shadows of silence.

For many of us, family rules, whether spoken or unspoken, have conditioned us to keep certain secrets. The inner critic keeps reminding us of these rules: "Don't talk about what really happened, and don't talk about what sets us apart from other people. Don't talk about our pain; we are trying to forget it ourselves. Help us pretend that everything is all right, because it hurts too much."

We have talked about the dynamics of the family, its rules and myths. You may understand why the family wants you to keep silent, but as we work to heal ourselves, we need to come to terms with the voices of the silencers.

Silence feeds shame. The antidote to the critic is to speak out, to state your truth out loud and in writing, to step out of the shadows instead of hiding in the darkness where shame flourishes.

In order to be free to speak our truths, we all need to create a safe place in our heads and with our writing community. First, we learn to listen to ourselves, and then we learn how to share with others. Using awareness, writing exercises, and sheer determination, we can learn how to overcome those inner voices and free ourselves to write what is true for us.

We have already explored the issue of telling the truth, facing the facts, and feeling freer to have our own points of view. The inner critic is a direct roadblock in the way of doing this. If we don't silence the silencers, our writing suffers along with our souls. Become conscious of the whisperings of the critic. See if you can discover the origins of those voices in your family rules, roles, and myths.

Some inner critic voices:

- No one will be interested.
- Who else cares about what happened?
- People will get mad at me.
- Who do you think you are?
- I am boring.
- I can't write.
- I'm not really a writer.
- I'm too ashamed to put this on paper.
- What if my memories are wrong?
- I don't really know the truth.
- My family will hate me and/or disown me.
- They know best about what happened.
- It will kill them if I write this.

Freeing Ourselves to Speak Out

The inner critic is tenacious. You probably already know how strong this voice can be, how strident and intrusive. It can paralyze beginning writers, and my students talk about it with me frequently. They want to know how get rid of it. Sometimes they tell me they don't want to read or share because secretly the critic is yelling at them.

The good and bad news is that the critical voice is a part of you. To get more acquainted with your inner critic, write a dialogue with it. When it says, "You're stupid, you can't write," ask, "Who taught me this? Where did this belief come from?"

If the voice says, "You're stupid. What makes you think you can write such a long work?" you can answer back, "Well, it's true that I don't know everything, and I was bad in [fill in the blank subject in school]. But I have written some things that seemed to say what I wanted them to, and even [fill in the name of a friend, editor, teacher, family member] liked it."

Keep a list of the negative phrases you hear in your head for a few weeks, then read them over and decide how to counter each of them with a positive, assertive statement. Some will simply melt away after being acknowledged.

Often you can see that the negative phrase is the voice of a parent or other family member. For example, if the voice says, "Don't you dare tell," you can respond with, "I am not telling to embarrass you or to be mean. I just need to tell this story. It has bothered me for years."

If the voice says, "You're going to kill someone if you write that," you can answer, "You have used guilt to control me for years, but now this is my private project, and I need to do it. I am exercising my autonomy by telling my truth."

When the inner critic bothers you while you're writing, take a separate piece of paper and write down what it says, then put the paper aside and return to your writing. If the critical voice begins again, stop to write down what it says. Try not to judge or analyze it at that time; just go back to your story.

Building Strength through Writing

Earlier I talked about the need to be witnessed as an important part of the healing process. We need two kinds of witnesses—internal and external. The internal witness is the compassionate part of ourselves, which we can strengthen through practice. When we listen deeply to ourselves and give ourselves sympathy, forgiveness, and comfort, a deep healing takes place. By not allowing the inner critic to keep shaming us and by refuting its statements, we learn not to shrink and crumble in the face of criticism.

If you were criticized and shamed during childhood—and most of us were to varying degrees, by the family or by the world—it was impossible to talk back. To do so was dangerous, so we learned to internalize those voices and keep silent.

Because this is learned behavior, we can unlearn it. Dealing with your inner critic and claiming your own voice is profoundly healing. As you do so, you learn to be your own witness and you build creative muscles.

Keep these guidelines in mind as you dismantle your inner critic and become your own compassionate witness:

- Be patient.
- Have compassion for yourself.
- Keep writing.
- Commit yourself to healing your past conditioning by work ing with the Writing Invitations at the end of this chapter.

How to work with the critic

In a writing group or other safe place, talk about what your inner critic says. Sharing the "bad" voices in your head and getting them out into the open is an important healing tool.

Another way to work with the inner critic is to write a letter addressing it directly about what it does to you. Write about its power, the pain it causes, and how it frustrates you. Sometimes, the critical voice was born in English class or because of a harsh teacher. If you suffered humiliation when you expressed yourself in school, write down the phrases you remember. For example, "You always got the worst grade in spelling, and you always failed your essays."

Share these statements with your group and use new phrases and beliefs to contradict the negative, critical ones. For example, "This is not about getting good grades. I am no longer fourteen years old. I have learned to write well enough, and I can hire an editor if I want. Shut up and let me write."

Or, if you truly feel that your work is not as good as you would like it to be, try this approach: "I would like to improve my writing, and I don't think it meets my standards yet, but it is not bad, I am not bad. I am learning. I need time to practice this new skill. Critic, please allow me to do this without putting me down. Allow me to learn at my own pace."

Affirmations and positive thinking are another way to move beyond the critic voice. Meditations and affirmations that are designed to help you with your writing path are in Appendix A.

When I began to write, my critic was harsh and I always felt ashamed when I showed my work to people, even when they said they liked it. I thought I was alone. I thought no one else suffered like that. Then, as I listened to published authors talk about their writing process, I discovered "real" authors had this demon too, and they wrote and published their books anyway. I found that the way to heal the critic trap was to write and write, continuing doggedly through the levels of shame, hoping that it would get easier some day.

It is easier now. The solution to my suffering was to face the page and to write my story, to not let my inner critic silence me. You can do that too. Keep writing. Face the critic, work with it, and write your story.

Writing Invitations

1. Write down what the critic-censor says as a way of downloading those voices out of your head.

2. Answer each accusation in writing. For example, if the inner critic says "You are boring," write your response: "Some people are interested in what I write, so what you say isn't true." Answer the critic as you would a person who was attacking you.

3. Write down some truths you're supposed to keep secret. What does the critic say to you during this exercise?

4. Write a story you are not supposed to write. Listen to the critic as you write it and answer back on a separate piece of paper.

5. Write down at least five secrets that you have kept all your life. What does your inner critic say in response?

6. What stories are you never going to write? Create a list.

7. What is truth—yours vs. that of another member of your family? Use dialogue to write a scene expressing opposing truths.

8. Make a list of specific people who would tell you to be quiet and quit writing. What would they say? Write it all down and then answer back to them. Share this with your trusted writing group.

9. Keep journaling about the inner critic, and keep writing!

14

The Ethics of Writing True Stories

I tore myself away from the safe comfort of certainties through my love for truth – and truth rewarded me.

—Simone de Beauvoir

Writing a memoir inevitably brings up ethical dilemmas: how much to write about family secrets, how much truth to tell. Each family member sees and remembers events differently. Many families live for years with a shaky truce about what "really" happened—a truce that is shattered when a family member writes and publishes a memoir. There's nothing like the printed word to stir up family disagreements.

Blackbird and *Still Waters,* memoirs by Jennifer Lauck, were published to great critical acclaim. Lauck is the only remaining member of her original family. In *Blackbird,* the narrator is a seven-year-old child who presents her feelings about complex living arrangements and decisions that profoundly affect her life. In the story, she is very young when her mother dies, and her father remarries soon after. *Still Waters* continues her story into adolescence and adulthood, as she revisits childhood mysteries and fills in other layers of the story.

After publication of *Blackbird,* Lauck found herself embroiled in a disagreement with her stepmother and stepsiblings, who accused her of lying and presenting incidents that make them look bad. When and under what circumstances the relationship between Lauck's father and stepmother developed is one of the matters disputed by the stepfamily. Salon.com published an article about the conflict. Lauck defended her work, saying, ". . .this is the memory of a little girl, and I wrote it to the best of my ability, and I stand behind it 100 percent."

Other stories are in the public media, from the James Frey shaming by Oprah to questions about other memoirists. The stories of most memoir writers have been questioned by the media, family members, or the public, leaving the memoir writer feeling vulnerable and questioning what to put on the page. The press seems to seize on the issue of truth in writing, to the dismay of the authors who make considered decisions about how they present their stories and how much "fictionalizing" they must do to create a work of art. The issue of whether your writing will please or anger family members, or the public if it is published, lies at the heart of each memoir writer's conscience.

The memoirist worries about being accused of terrible things by the family—betrayal, disloyalty, and narcissism. Some stories in the memoir may no longer be hot subjects for the writer, but other family members may not have resolved them.

Family disagreements bring up guilt and shame in the memoir writer. The writer may worry:

• How dare I think this or say that? I love my parents. They have changed; we've worked it out. I feel guilty writing about what really happened.
• I don't want to bring back up the past. I am afraid of those feelings.
• I have already talked about it endlessly in therapy. I don't understand why I can't just forget it, but the memories haunt me day and night in dreams.
• I feel guilty and ashamed.

Memory or Fact?

You can't prove a memory. You can never prove what happened or didn't happen. Several years ago a court case in California that involved memories made the front pages. A woman reported a flashback about her father killing one of her childhood friends. On the basis of this recovered memory, the father was tried and found guilty. He was freed upon appeal on the basis that the memory was influenced by hypnosis and therapy.

Many families have been torn asunder by painful accusations made as a result of recovered memories. The person making the accusation says the memory was recovered during the process of therapy, and that it had been repressed for years. The judicial system does not want to send people to jail based on something that can't be proved. According to the law, a memory is not an objective fact.

As a therapist, I know that memories can suddenly appear and cause great psychic trauma for the client. What the client does about it becomes part of the therapy. Whether the memory is "true" or not isn't our focus; instead, we work on how to heal the wounds that are now part of the person's conscious experience.

So it is with memoir writing. Family members can object strenuously to certain stories in a memoir, insisting that they simply aren't true. "That never happened, you are making it up." Your justified defense is, "This is the way I see it. This is what happened to me." Some family members have borrowed memories. I've heard brothers and sisters insist that what one remembers actually happened to the other one.

To complete your memoir, you'll need to decide what memory means to you. The simplest way is to write what you remember as clearly and as well as you can. As you write, your memory may shift, or more memories may arise from your unconscious. Keep a dream journal and an open mind.

For the first few months, focus on writing your stories without getting the family involved. After you have worked for a while, you may have a better idea of what to say and what not to say to the family about the content of your writing. If you are writing about events and situations that you know will bring shame and guilt, it is important for your own healing that you complete the writing before confronting family members with it.

Secrets

It is safe to say that there are no families without secrets or conflicts. Some writers choose to go along with the family rules and keep the silence; others want to explore deeper truths, believing that exposure heals the wounds that secrets and lies create. No one can tell you what you should or should not reveal in your memoir. Perhaps you feel that, knowing your family as you do, there are some issues which should not be discussed.

As a memoir writer, you must ask yourself:

- Who will be injured if I write this?
- Is there a purpose to writing this; will there be a healing?

As a memoir writer, you must come to terms with your own position. Remember: The first draft is for your own healing. Secrets hold danger, like the submerged part of an iceberg, and they have a profound effect on those who keep them. Energy is required to cover up secrets, so they often feel like heavy burdens.

Telling secrets has always caused controversy in our society. For instance, victims are often afraid to speak out about harassment or sexual abuse by family members, priests, teachers, bosses, or anyone in a position of authority. A secret holds power; the person keeping it can completely change another person's life by revealing it. Often a great deal is at stake—reputations, jobs, economic well-being, family unity, and most of all, the way the family sees itself. As a result, the life of the person who tells the secret may never be the same afterwards.

James Framo is a family therapist who invites the family of origin to therapy sessions to help resolve couple conflicts. During a training workshop, he said that every couple resisted having the family come in: "It will kill them. They'll never speak to me again. My dad will have a heart attack."

In every case, none of these dire events occurred. The secret, the anger, the stuck place was gently discussed, opening up communication in the family for the first time. Our worst fears may come from our child self, and are usually unfounded in current reality.

One writer I know had a positive attitude about his memoir. He believed that the information he told in it was already known and understood by his family—it wasn't a secret. He had omitted the worst details and secrets from his story so he wouldn't violate privacy rights or defame anyone's character. But suddenly, this writer, whose nuclear family was dead, was shunned by the extended family. A cousin told him that various family members were gossiping about him because of a few innocuous paragraphs that had gotten around. These paragraphs were combed for possible insults, and insults were found even where they were not intended. The family was clearly worried about what secret "sins" might be uncovered.

The writer didn't receive criticism of himself or his work directly, even when he asked for it. The family pretended that everything was all right, depriving the writer of the chance to set the record straight, to provide reassurance, even to have any discussion about his stories. He came to understand that the family's reaction was part of a longstanding pattern of indirect communication, gossip, and power positioning—and that he could do nothing to stop it.

Even when we write what we think are positive things about family members, they may interpret our words as they wish and may still become angry or upset with us.

As I wrote and rewrote my own memoir, I decided that despite a negative reaction from my extended family, I had to continue. I did not disclose most of the family secrets because they weren't necessary to the story I chose to write. But the fact that I have written a memoir created a kind of paranoia: "What is she saying? Is it about us?"

Writing Their Stories—Finding Compassion

When I began my memoir, I found that I still had to face the anger and pain I held about certain events in my life. I faced my grandmother as she screamed at me from inside my head. As I kept telling the truth the way I had experienced it, I gradually let go of layers of anger, sorrow, and fear. I learned to differentiate myself from her, and became more real to myself.

To develop more compassion for her, I began writing the story of my grandmother as a young woman. I stood in the shoes of a sixteen-year-old girl who had eloped in 1911, a young woman who had given birth to a stillborn child in 1914, and then to my mother in 1915. I imagined her pain and heartache as I wrote those stories through her eyes.

I felt that I was healing not only myself, but her, as well. She had not been able to tell the truth; her fear, anxiety, and mental illness prevented that. By telling her stories, I was able to free myself—and perhaps psychically, my grandmother—from the past. This was an aspect of my ethics—to try to create more compassion, to attempt to heal decades of pain and rage. I could not do it directly, but I could do it in the writing.

Writing Ethically

After you have written a few drafts of your family stories, think about the issues that concern you. Did you reveal any family secrets or expose any subjects you fear you could be sued for? Could your writing cause a huge family uproar? What is most important, the family or the writing? Consider the ethical dilemmas that need to be resolved before your memoir is published.

Just because we *can* say certain things does not mean it is a good idea to say them. Just because we might not be sued or have legal action brought against us does not mean that we should put questionable or "hot" information into words. In the final stages of writing, you must decide whether or not to include potentially damaging or upsetting material in your memoir.

One of my students, Denise, tells how she struggled with how these issues in her memoir:

On Writing the Truth about Loved Ones

By Denise Roessle

I'm constantly wrestling with how much truth to reveal about family and friends who are still alive. During my pregnancy, I lived with a woman who had an enormous heart and a huge drinking problem. I witnessed a lot over those seven months, and while it's not all relevant to my story, some of it is. We became friends and still are, 32 years later. I worry that portraying her honestly will hurt her, and I find myself going back over that part of the story, looking for ways to soften it without totally sacrificing the truth.

With my parents, who played a major role in what happened, it's even worse. A little voice in my head says: "These people aren't monsters. It couldn't have been that bad. They love you, and what you're doing is going to kill them." I envision them completely cutting me off once the book is out, and my sister and brother being angry with me for spilling my guts in public. Sometimes I catch myself wishing that they were already dead so I wouldn't have to worry about their reactions.

I don't want to hurt anybody, but I need to tell my story, to say the truth and be heard. For once, I'm making my needs more important than everyone else's. I'm going ahead with it, letting the chips fall where they may. That decision alone has been a major step toward healing.

Revenge

Getting revenge is not the best motivation for writing a memoir. If you have been wounded, writing about your feelings is a good way to resolve them. Writing the stories about what happened can help you come to a new understanding. But writing to get back at others almost always backfires. I heard a published memoir writer describe his many complaints about what happened to him after his memoir came out: he was sued, and his family was shocked and hurt at what he wrote. He had not warned the people involved about the content of his work, however, and much of it was angry and highly judgmental. He had hoped they would never find out about his book because he had changed his name. He said the memoir had created another level of conflict and hurt feelings, but he seemed to have no idea how this had happened.

You are the only one who can decide whether putting the "truth"—your version of it—out into the world will help create a healing experience for you and your family. Ask yourself if you have a fantasy that after your memoir is written there will be an upsurge in family forgiveness, or that longstanding grudges will suddenly dissolve once you present your point of view, which you believe is the correct one.

It may be hard to predict how the memoir will affect family and friends. All you can do is to be as ethical and compassionate as possible when you present your work to the family and the public. Being ethical does not mean that you agree with what other members of the family think or that you have to be close or connected. Being ethical means that you protect yourself and your work, and that you maintain proper boundaries when sharing your opinion, which after all is what a memoir is, with the larger world.

Here are some topics to consider and some suggestions that will help you to behave ethically in regard to your memoir:

• Are there serious grudges or emotional cutoffs with family and friends?

• Do you want to *ask permission* or do you want to *tell* your family what you are writing about? "Asking permission" means making a request that can be denied. This affects what you write about and how you write it. Be clear before you speak about your intentions or make your requests.

• Be prepared to negotiate sticky issues.

• If you mention real names, get permission to use them. After you write your piece, show it to the people named and obtain their written consent before putting it in print.

• If your piece reveals information about a town or any public figures or events, be sure that your facts are accurate before publishing.

• Make certain that you are not defaming anyone's character or invading his privacy. Check with a literary attorney to see what these terms mean. If you have a publisher, the staff and attorneys will work with you on this, but if you publish independently, you need to take care of it yourself.

• Be sure that you do not express your opinions as facts. As you do your research, check as many facts as possible.

• If non-family members are included in the book, be willing to change names, physical descriptions, and the locations of towns or other public arenas.

• Fictionalizing, changing certain things to protect the guilty and the innocent, may be necessary when preparing for publication. It may be a good idea to state in your introduction that changes were made in the literal truth for these reasons.

• Publishing a memoir means considering it as a public literary endeavor. Put aside any concerns you may have about publishing until you complete a full draft of the memoir. As with any public statement, ethical issues arise and must be solved. Ideally, the solutions will allow the work to be healing for everyone involved.

Writing Invitations

1. What emotional reactions are you concerned will occur when you present your memoir to family? What are your top five worries about what will happen? Write about those worries.

2. Think about revenge. Is there anyone you'd like to get back at? Do you imagine someone reading your memoir and feeling sorry or apologizing to you? Write about this in your journal.

3. Will your family think your work is fair and balanced?

4. List any memoir-related ethical problems that concern you.

5. How do you feel about taking your memoir into the public arena? Journal about this as you go through the process of writing and publishing your memoir.

6. If you want your work published, research your rights and your legal and ethical responsibilities.

15

 Forgiveness

Forgiveness means letting go of the past.
—Gerald Jampolsky

*M*oments of trauma or regret may surface as you write your memoir. You may encounter unfinished business with someone in your family or with a friend from the past. Looking at who you once were and at the kinds of relationships you had at different times in your life can stimulate a new awareness of injuries done to you, or wounds you may have inflicted on others, intentionally or unintentionally. As you reflect, you may find that you need to bring certain relationships into balance through a process of forgiveness—either by asking for it or by forgiving someone else.

Everyone has vulnerabilities and emotional triggers. What would be an insult to one person is not to another but, again, a memoir seems to bring up an awareness of hurts and secrets from the past. How dare you (or Aunt Josie) talk about Sara's abortion, Bob's drunken girlfriend, or great-grandma's secret second marriage. When the war starts, people take sides and create opposing factions, setting up dynamics that go on for years and even cross into the next generation, which is expected to continue the war out of loyalty. Walls are built that are hard to break down.

How, then, can forgiveness occur? The process involves two points of view: the person requesting forgiveness and the person being asked for it. Forgiveness can be sought in person or through writing. Sometimes it can be accomplished only *in absentia*, as when the other party is deceased or out of reach. And there may be times when you would prefer to resolve your feelings without confronting the other person directly, when you want to put your feelings aside, to forgive even if you don't forget, and move on.

Forgiving an action does not mean acknowledging it as acceptable or no longer considering it an injury or injustice. Forgiving does not necessarily mean forgetting. What has been done can't be undone; forgiveness does not mean that it didn't happen. It does not undo anything.

Forgiveness means that you stop feeling resentment. Forgiveness means that your energy is freed up. When you let go of the resentment, you are free to move on with your life. If you desire forgiveness, it means that you are trying to bring balance to your life, realign your ethics, and let go of guilt and shame. This lightens emotional burdens and enables both parties to move on and live more positive lives.

Forgiveness Through Unsent Letters

If you have been injured by the behavior of another, write a letter stating directly and in exact detail the time, place, physical location—the entire scene—of what happened, how it happened, and your conclusions about it. Write how you felt about yourself and the other person. Be thorough and specific. State each event, each action, and each reaction from your point of view.

Write this letter to the person you feel injured by, but do not send it. Put it aside in your journal or another private place. You may have to write several versions to get everything said the way you need to say it.

Then write a letter about this injury to a best friend, either someone you knew at the time, who was familiar with the situation, or to a current friend. When you focus your words toward a specific person, you focus your thoughts and emotions. Write this letter as many times as you need to. Don't cut this process short. Continue to write different versions until you feel you have nothing more to say.

Now switch roles. Stand in the shoes of the person you feel injured by. First, write the response you expect he or she would give you in person. Next, write the response you want to receive from that person, whether or not you feel he or she will give it to you. Write what you want to hear; write what you need to hear. Write this response as often as you need to.

A Forgiveness Conversation

If you are the petitioner, the one asking for forgiveness from someone you have injured, it helps to:

• Acknowledge the other person's feelings with empathy, saying something like, "I understand it hurt your feelings when I . . ."

• Apologize and ask for forgiveness, but only if you are sincere about it. Clearly say, "I am sorry. Please forgive me." This needs to be a genuine response from your heart, and you must realize that the other person may not choose to respondpositively. You are taking an emotional risk. Do not expect that the other person will grant forgiveness immediately. It may take time.

• Don't make excuses. Any explanation can slide into an excuse, which takes away from the apology.

If you are being asked for forgiveness:

• Express what hurt you, and be specific.

•If you are angry, choose words that state your anger clearly.

• Ask if the other person understands what you are saying; have the other person repeat your communication back to you.

• Consider your response carefully. If you can't genuinely forgive the person, don't pretend and don't be dishonest. Although the petitioner may have waited a long time to request forgiveness, don't feel pressured to forgive unless you really mean it.

• If you do feel that you can forgive, express yourself clearly. Communicate your understanding or empathy. Forgiveness is a great gift. By giving it, you bring balance back to the relationship.

Writing Invitations

1. Write about an injury that you feel you can't forgive. Write very specifically—who, what, when, where, how. Use sensual details.

2. Write about why you can't forgive an injury or the person who committed it. Over a period of time, write several versions, first for ten minutes and then for twenty minutes, until you feel you have expressed all your feelings about it.

3. Think about how you have hurt another person. Write a story giving details about that person, how you knew each other, what was good about the relationship, and the circumstances of the injustice or injury you caused. How do you understand yourself in that situation? Would you act differently now?

4. Write the story with a new plot. How could it turn out differently? What skills, understanding, or emotional knowledge do you have now that you did not have then? Have you asked for forgiveness from that person? Can you forgive yourself?

5. How did your family act when it came to grudges and forgiveness? Write family stories about forgiveness. Be sure to describe the "characters," your family members, using sensual details—color, sound, smell, and tactile sensations. Use action and dialogue to show what happened.

16

Love and Happiness

> *Love and compassion are necessities, not luxuries.*
> *Without them humanity cannot survive.*
>
> —Dalai Lama

ove is one of the most important qualities in human life. It is often the most difficult to define or to write about, but we all know what it is.

The word "love" is used to talk about romantic love, a great dinner, a friendship, or our affection for a pet. The kinds of love we feel and want to express are as varied as snowflakes. Love describes a wide range of experiences, from great bear hugs to looking into the eyes of our beloved, from dark chocolate to unity with God and nature. To some, love is petting a cat or dog, spring rain, snow on bare trees, exalting music. Love is the healing force in the universe, shining its light into dark corners. Love is expansive and empathic; it understands and gathers in the lost and lonely. Love is connection and beauty, acceptance and courage. Love is the opposite of fear. It is like a prism, each facet reflecting a different color of light.

When we write and talk about family, the complexity and the conflicts of love become apparent. Love is a word that has become complicated with need, desperation, and selfishness, but it is really about expansion and deep appreciation. Think about who and what you love. See if you can expand your range of love.

"True love is the intention and capacity to offer joy and happiness," writes Thich Nhat Hanh, a Vietnamese Buddhist monk and prolific author. The highest, most unselfish kind of love, according to psychologists and spiritual teachers, is unconditional love. To love unconditionally means to love with no expectation of return. This may be difficult, at times even impossible, but we can practice it by becoming aware of our neediness or our tendency to "give in order to get."

The Dalai Lama speaks about love and happiness in his book *The Art of Happiness*. If we want to practice the simplicity of love and happiness, and thereby counter the darker forces in the world, we can practice feeling love in our hearts at least once each day, as well as happiness.

Love contains and encompasses all the other aspects: joy, equanimity, and compassion. A sense of equanimity offers balance and full presence, the awareness of self and other. Equanimity is love that gives without guilt or possession, admires without envy or greed and receives without demand for reciprocation. "If your love has attachments, discrimination, prejudice, or clinging in it, it is not true love," he says.

When we practice equanimity, there is balance, empathy, and compassion in our dealings with others, offering us a peaceful way of being with ourselves and our loved ones. We may need to practice this, one moment at a time. Each time we feel prejudice or judgment, we can practice letting it go.

Hanh defines compassion as "the intention and capacity to relieve and transform suffering and lighten sorrow." Compassion literally means "to suffer with," but we don't need to suffer to help relieve suffering. We show concern when we are compassionate, opening our hearts to a deep understanding of the other person, his trials, needs, and stuck places. We do not, and cannot, fix his problems, but by acceptance and our own full presence we can provide deep comfort.

"With compassion in our heart, every thought, word and deed can bring about a miracle," says Hanh.

When we have compassion, we feel a deep connection with humanity and with our own wounds. To have compassion is to be a whole human being, striving to find life in balance. When we feel the lack of compassion, we have the opportunity to put ourselves in the position of the one we judge and ask how we would like to be treated. All of us are imperfect and suffer. All of us need to receive and give compassion, and in so doing our hearts are released into joy.

It is with joy that we embrace the beauty of the world, green trees, ocean spray, birdsong, the purr of a cat. The look on the face of a happy baby is pure joy. It is natural to feel joy and to receive it. Joy bubbles up like a stream, spills over, and is contagious. Joy is within us and shines through us. Joy can be the thing that helps us to move forward in the delicious tasting of what life has to offer.

There are many moments of joy, equanimity, and compassion that in our remembering give us a second blessing as we write about them. Joy appears in the world, and in the silences of our own hearts.

Love and the Eye of the Beholder

You must define for yourself what love means and decide how you will carry on family traditions and beliefs about love in your life and through your writing. Family members may agree or disagree about what love is. To one it might mean unselfish giving; to another it could mean mowing the lawn, baking a pie, or cutting someone's hair. Love can be physical, emotional, free or extremely costly. It can be a challenge to write about emotions, and we have already discussed writing about both the dark and the lighter events in life. Because some of our stories may have painful subjects, thinking about moments of love—when love, joy or compassion made a difference in the family—gives us an opportunity to heal.

A negative family cycle can be broken by an extraordinary event, such as a natural disaster, the death of a family member, a birth, a marriage, or some other event so striking that it breaks through bitterness and grudges, roles and myths. Sometimes an innocent child unites a split family finally able to they see through fresh eyes the old patterns of the past. A single person can break through patterns and unconscious conditioning, creating a new form and destiny for the future. It is in our families that we test our skills, try out our developing personality; and it is to the enfolding family with its unconditional love that, if we are lucky, we can return.

Non-Standard Families

The protective wings of the birth family may not be available to a child who has been abandoned, denied, or orphaned. Some children who have been raised by non-blood family or extended family feel that they have been cared for more than they would have been in their family of origin.

If your family has been fragmented, writing stories about it can help unite the broken strands in yourself. As the narrator who observes with perspective, you can use this weaving to heal ancient, deep wounds, to create an identity that holds and a matrix that can contain and comfort.

Most families, however defined, have a wealth of resources to balance problems and difficult issues. Human beings are capable of immense acts of generosity and kindness, altruistic love, and acts of beauty that transcend and transform pain and hurt. Such acts are part of the natural healing process in our lives, changing anger and depression to hope and success.

When you examine your family's history, you may discover inspiring stories of courage, love, generosity, and strength. The positive qualities of our ancestors can be gifts for us to draw on. We can be inspired by a great-great aunt who walked behind a Conestoga wagon for three thousand miles, or a grandfather who managed to feed his family during the Great Depression, or acts of bravery and sacrifice during wartime. These kinds of stories galvanize our energy and make us want to carry on these traditions and qualities in our own lives. And they make wonderful stories for our memoirs.

In every family there are tales of spirituality, love, miracles, and blessings. We must remember that a necessary part of our healing is to discover and write our positive stories of happiness, joy, and love. It is in these stories that we find sparks of understanding to inspire us to live our lives fully and richly, with a feeling of blessing.

Writing Invitations

1. How did your family show or define **love**? Think about the small acts as well as the larger ones. What acts of love do you hold close to your heart?

2 Make a list of people, or pets, who love you. Make a list of what and whom you love.

3. How was **loyalty** defined in your family; how were you loyal? How much was loyalty valued in your family? Write a story that shows family loyalty in action.

4. How did your family demonstrate **generosity**? Through gifts, actions, words? Whose generosity did you admire, and how do you show generosity?

5. How do you define **compassion**? Who was the most compassionate member of your family? Write a story that shows compassion in scene and dialogue.

6. Heart (*coeur*) is the root of **courage,** the ability to act in the face of danger or threat. How do you define courage? Write about courage in your life or the lives of others you admire.

7. **Tolerance** is the ability to stretch emotional resources and accept differences. How has tolerance been shown or not shown in your family?

8. **Creativity** and creative expression includes gardening, sewing, building cars or houses, crafts, the arts, painting, knitting, and hobbies. In what ways do you and your family show creativity? Make lists of important creative activities in your life.

Writing the Memoir

As we reveal ourselves in story, we become aware of the continuing core of our lives under the fragmented surface of our experience. . . . Most important, as we become aware of ourselves as storytellers, we realize that what we understand and imagine about ourselves is a story. And when we know all this, we can use our stories to heal and make ourselves whole.

—Susan Wittig Albert
*Writing from Life:
Telling Your Soul's Story*

17

The Process of Writing

...imagination needs moodling—long,
inefficient, happy idling,
dawdling and puttering.

—Brenda Ueland

*W*hen you write a memoir, you invite reflections and dreams. When you are in *reverie*—the French word for dream—you are in a right-brain, nonlinear world, a poetic world of images and associations. To enhance our creativity we need to allow our brain to dream and remain unfocused. Many people say that after trying unsuccessfully to solve a problem, they engage in some unrelated activity—taking a shower, baking a pie, cleaning the house (writers tend to have some of the cleanest houses in the world)—and afterwards they find their problems solved. The right brain works holistically and needs to be unburdened from directed, logical thinking.

Brenda Ueland suggests taking long meditative walks to allow the mind to wander. Inspiration often comes in this way.

Stages of Creative Writing

Just as a flower evolves from a seed to green leafiness, then to a larger plant with mature blossoms, so your memoir will grow in stages.

Planting Seeds: Follow your idea, your spark, an image that presents itself. Write in your journal. Don't censor your work. Do the Writing Invitations in this book. Create a folder of vignettes. Work on your timeline (see Chapter 18). Put questions about publishing aside until later. I have seen students get stuck writing their memoir by trying to sell the book before it is written. Most first-time authors need to finish their book before anyone will take a serious look at it, though surprises do happen. If you are working on your first book, you won't know how it will turn out until you have written at least a full first draft. So be patient and surrender to the writing process.

Using the Right Tools: In this stage you make time to write. Create a schedule, several small segments of time each week to write. Write as often as you can, either in your journal or for your memoir. Attend readings to hear other writers' work, and attend writing conferences. You may want to join a writing group. This stage requires that you listen deeply to your story; it also requires the motivation to continue to write the painful stories. Keep your inner critic at bay. It may be helpful to do the Writing Invitations about the inner critic at the end of Chapter 13. They will encourage an open, positive frame of mind.

Tending: During this stage you track the stories that you know need to be included in your book. Keep a list of the stories you have written and another of the ones you intend to write. There is a synchronicity to this process. Someone else's story that you hear in your writing group may spark a memory for you. Reading published memoirs is a good way to learn about structure, writing style, and story, and it may stimulate ideas of your own. At this time you may also want to do genealogical research, visit relatives, and talk to siblings.

Designing: In this stage the book begins to take shape. You can see a narrative line or theme that weaves through it. You organize the parts and make decisions about what stays in the book. You think about ethical issues, the questions about family and privacy. Quilting, organizing and reorganizing the parts, may continue throughout the first and later drafts.

Pruning: Begin editing and rewriting. Look closely to see what the book really needs, what it is really about, and how to focus the themes. You will need to think again about your ideas and concepts, and then perhaps perform a heavy revision of your text. Michelangelo once described his work as releasing the sculpture from the marble; this applies to writing a book, as well. During this stage, you release one story from the multitude of possible stories you could include.

Harvesting: It is time to engage the services of a professional editor to help smooth the text and prepare it for publication. At the same time, inform your family or friends that you have written about them, and ask them to read what you have said. Your role changes now from writer to marketer. You must decide whether to get an agent, whether you can find a publisher on your own, or whether you want to self-publish.

Safe Writing Groups

A writing group is helpful during the long process of writing a memoir, but it needs to be the right group, ideally one that focuses on memoir. When my students have joined fiction groups, they have felt vulnerable because their personal stories are exposed as real and authentic while other members are protected because the stories they share are fictional. Unless the group you have joined focuses on writing as an act of healing, and unless the group understands family dynamics and the vulnerability of writing about it, you may hear unhelpful comments and judgments, such as, "That can't be true; that could never happen; oh, come on, you're exaggerating. That's crazy, how could you let that happen to you." One group I attended scathingly (and erroneously) talked about "stupid women who stayed in abusive relationships for the money." It was not safe to write about such relationships, especially in memoir form, in that group.

Be careful when you share stories about violence, mental illness, and other controversial social issues. People who have not been in therapy or who are uneducated about the complex dynamics of a dysfunctional family may find it difficult to understand such elements of the human condition. Sometimes powerful stories upset a member in the group who is in denial or unaware of his own buried wounds.

Women can feel they struggle to find or maintain their point of view and voice in a writing group attended by men. Although their published work will be read by both sexes, during the sensitive, early, creative process, many women may prefer feedback and support from women only. In 1997, Susan Wittig Albert formed the Story Circle Network, which offers online groups, a quarterly journal, and ways that women can create a supportive local writing network. Please visit them online at www.storycircle.org.

A supportive writing group will provide more useful and objective information about your work than your friends and family can. Well-intentioned friends and family members frequently give nonobjective feedback based on how they feel about you. Because spouses and friends don't want you to feel bad when you're writing painful stories, they may suggest that you give it up. The people who love you do not want you to cry, struggle, or feel pain. "Just let it go," they say. "Just stay in the present and forget it." Under pressure you may feel tempted to give up your project. Moments of pain do occur along the way to healing. It's a good idea to protect your writing and yourself by joining a supportive writing group, and keeping your work private from the world. The wrong feedback can kill your work in its infancy.

Here's what one of my students, Robin Malby, wrote about her experience:

> *Participating in a memoir-writing group has given me a great deal of healing and encouragement as a beginning writer. My stories center around my journey from a life of chronic pain and illness to a state of improved health and spiritual strength. They are not easy stories to write because they require that I call up unpleasant and often traumatic memories and put them into words. I have found*

that the process of revisiting those dark days of pain and illness and putting those experiences on paper allows an additional layer of sadness and trauma to be released, physically and emotionally.

What is most healing for me is reading my stories aloud to the group, whose members have come to serve as a circle of supportive witnesses. What I discovered on my journey to wellness was that dynamic people and committed healers come in all different kinds of packages, some being not at all what one would expect. Being able to bring these individuals to life on the written page and receive feedback from my writing group has encouraged me to keep writing.

Keeping a Journal

Because healing is the purpose of writing your memoir, record your feelings about your memoir writing in a journal. You may record ideas, fears, worries about what your family will say about a particular story—anything that helps you keep your stories alive and your voice engaged in the stories you are telling. You may find yourself living in the in-between world of present and past, and keeping a journal helps you to keep track of this back and forth process.

For some writers, making the transition from "now" to "then" is as easy as closing their eyes; for others it is like standing on the edge of a pool deciding when to jump into cold water. The journal not only allows you to process your feelings about writing, It gives you a place to record the whisperings of new stories. And it helps you to keep the habit of writing regularly, even if your stories are not ready for the page.

Finding Time for Writing

Writing makes demands on your time, and thrives if there is a routine. My students tell me, "I didn't have time to write this week. I was dreaming and thinking about the story, but I don't have anything to show for it."

I reassure them that they're engaged in their work, even when musing. A memoir writer needs to spend time thinking, dreaming, musing, and keeping a journal. A story must live inside you, and you must learn to listen it out—to listen deeply and with full presence—in order to bring it out of your body. Accepting your process and your Self assists in this listening-out stage.

Because everyone's creative process works differently, you need to do what works for you. Louise DeSalvo, in *Writing as a Way of Healing*, suggests setting a firm time by which you decide when the work will be complete, and then counting backwards from there. To use this method, you figure out how long the project will take, how many hours a week you will write, how many hours a day, and how many pages per hour. Very disciplined, but this method does not work for everyone.

Some new writers set impossible goals for themselves: "I will write every day for two or three hours." They become unhappy when that impossible schedule can't be kept. They feel like failures, and want to give up. Still, most writers find that sticking to a writing schedule helps them feel good about their writing. Even a book-length memoir can be completed with steady but brief bursts of writing. You will be amazed at what you can accomplish in fifteen minutes.

So set realistic goals. If you have a job or have family to take care of, set aside just four twenty-minute blocks of time each week. After a while, when the writing begins to flow smoothly, you can increase the time you spend on it.

The creative process can't be rushed. You will discover a pattern that works for you. At times you may feel stuck. When that happens you'll come up with all sorts of excuses:

- *I can't write unless I have a three- or four-hour block of time.*
- *I can't write until I know what I am going to say.*
- *I'm afraid I'll feel bad afterwards.*
- *I'm depressed.*
- *I don't see why I should bother doing it.*

Remind yourself to approach the writing with beginner's mind: simply put your pen to the page and write. It doesn't matter what you say; just write. You can edit later. If you write only when you feel good and have lots of time, you miss the benefits of ongoing writing.

Vignettes

The complexities of real life make it difficult to sort out the many threads of your story: the multiple strands of action, conversation, and mood; the myriad emotional undertones. To simplify the task, you can approach your memoir by writing vignettes. Vignettes are short, one- to five-page stories about a single event, person, place, or thing. Each vignette contains the heart of a story that you can flesh out later, in your first draft. Vignettes are the discreet pieces that, when quilted together, compose a memoir.

A satisfying way to begin is to write vignettes about things that rouse your passion—memories that worry you or make you curious or angry. The energy of this "fire in the belly" can help you get going. Writing a vignette every few days makes you feel that you are making progress, and you are!

As you write the vignettes, don't listen to your worries or your inner critic. You can always edit your work later. For now, just put the words down as they come out. Listen to the creative, hopeful voice inside you: *I need to write this. I need to heal. I have a story that needs to be told.*

Quilting Together the First Draft

As you write your first draft, you will be quilting your vignettes together to set the structure for your memoir. By quilting together several vignettes that tell a fuller story, you create a chapter. And so, vignette by vignette, chapter by chapter, you create a book-length draft, a tale with plot, characters, themes, and emotional insight.

Using the elements of fiction—scene, narration, dialogue, point of view, and description—helps you to build each chapter. Your great-aunt, grandmother, father, and best friend become characters in the book. Remember, these people are strangers to the reader. To make them familiar, you will use writing techniques that capture their essence, feeling, and character.

You must translate your memory dream world into words and images. As you translate experience from your inner world to the outside, you will search for language to create a state of mind in the reader that matches the memory, sensation, and image within you. This is called creating verisimilitude, creating a believable world.

One of the foundations of a memoir is the storyteller's voice, the way you the narrator speak, think, feel, and express yourself. In a memoir, you are both the teller of the story and a character in the story, almost like a split self. The narrator is a detached observer who tells the story. The narrator has a point of view, usually expressed by the first person "I," sometimes by the third person "she" or "he." You describe what happened and how you felt, presenting your interpretation of events to the reader.

You might create a scene to show your grandmother's house and how the family gathered around at Christmas. You might describe the smell of the fireplace, how people dressed, the food they ate. You will probably use dialogue and character portraits to show how people interacted. As narrator, you present a whole world, yours, to the reader. A detailed, structured narrative requires you to be fully present.

Just as some movies begin with long shots that pan the location or setting and then focus in a window or down a street searching for a person or some action, you can start your story by setting the broad scene, describing the geographic location, and then focusing on your childhood home and a main character. By what that character does or says, the reader becomes engaged with the story and wants to hear it all. Alternatively, you may choose to do just the opposite: start with a detail and move out.

Sometimes it may feel as if you're taking dictation—you place your pen on the page and write as fast as you can. When you are lucky and blessed, the writing flows, but this does not always happen, even with an oft-published author. Sometimes there are hard days, days when you stare at a blank page or a computer screen. Out dribbles a sentence, or a few words. But each of these hard-won sentences is work that needs to be done, work that will lead to another blessing from the stream of consciousness. It is said that we must do the hard work for the blessings to come.

Most of your first draft may sound and look terrible on the page. You may be tempted to tear it up and throw it away. In *Bird by Bird,* Anne Lamott says that everyone writes "shitty first drafts." Lamott's bald statement has given many writers permission to write that first awkward draft without feeling guilty. Instead, they read her amusing and cheery chapter and laugh at hanging their participles and sloppy metaphors.

The inner critic may try to shame you into getting rid of writing that could be improved or an idea that was interesting but needed time to be clarified. The critic can be particularly savage when you write about shameful things, or areas of your life that bring up insecurities or questions about yourself. No matter how bad you think your writing is, never, never erase what you have written. Download it into a file labeled "saved stuff." Remember, all writing leads to more writing, and the "bad" writing always leads to better writing. When in doubt, read the writing that you feel is terrible to your group. It helps to let your group know how you feel, and let them reflect your work back to you to see how it can go forward.

Have faith. Keep writing.

Writing Invitations

1. What are five reasons not to write your memoir?

2. List six reasons to write it anyway.

3. Make a writing date with yourself to get started. Find a café where you won't be interrupted while you write a few vignettes.

4. Find a writing buddy and spend time together writing, then treat yourselves afterward.

5. Write one vignette a week.

6. Locate local writing classes and peer groups. Talk with members. Visit the group.

7. Read memoirs and books about writing to encourage you to write your stories.

18

 Organizing Your Work

As in the word remember, we remember, we bring together the parts, we integrate that which has been alienated or separated out.

—Deena Metzger

"There are so many stories. How do I begin?" That is the lament I often hear from students as they being to write their memoirs. After thinking about your story for a long time, perhaps for years, you have started writing, or at least you've decided to "begin to start." But as you think about it, chapter one could be chapter ten. Or you could start a hundred years ago and tell the story of a great-grandmother or grandfather. Or you could begin the story in the present and flash back.

Where and with what story is the best way to begin the family saga? How do you separate the layers of stories? How do you speak about healing if you don't present the events that created the need for healing? Organizing the memoir can be especially difficult when writers have to deal with patterns like alcoholism, abandonment, and abuse.

Beginners often feel daunted by the emotional responsibility of writing a memoir. This psychological burden can get in the way of figuring out how to begin and what to write first. Having a practical, left-brain solution helps to take away some of the angst in writing a memoir. One technique that my students have found helpful is the timeline.

The Timeline

The timeline is a simple way to organize your life stories. When you see the big picture, the whole story broken down into years and dates, it is easier to decide which vignettes to write and where they should go.

The timeline helps you see how your stories fit into linear time. You may want to make several timelines, one for your parents and grandparents, one for your own life, and another for your memoir, which may include only a portion of your life. Some memoirs cover decades and several generations; some memoirs tell the story of just a week or a month of real time.

Your timeline will help you keep track of what happened to you, to other members of your family, and to the community. We do not exist in a vacuum. Our lives and memories are tied to events in the larger world. Significant and dramatic historical events intersect with our lives. In my generation, a frequently asked question was: Where were you when President Kennedy was killed? Today September 11, 2001 is that kind of touchstone.

During both of these moments, time seemed to stop. The story of a nation's tragedy was linked to everyone's personal vignette of that day. You can use your timeline to chart events during those historical marking points that happened to you or a family member.

You can use the timeline on page 124 as a model for making your own. Write in the dates and your age, and label events in circles.

Tape several sheets of paper together or buy a pad of large paper from an art supply store. Draw a long horizontal line to represent linear time. Bold vertical lines demarcate segments of one, two, five, or ten years, depending on the nature of the particular timeline and how many details you want to include. Experiment. Use pencil so you can erase.

Vertical lines descending from the horizontal connect to the circles in which you will write a word or phrase to identify important events. Place a check mark or colored dot next to all the circles that name dark stories, the ones that would be painful to write.

Writing from Your Timelines

The words or phrases you've put in the circles are the working titles of your stories. Each one shows the core of a story, an important occasion, or a turning point.

From those working titles create a list of the stories you want to write. For each story, name the characters, the location, the date, and the significance of the story. Here's an example:

First Move

1. *Age 3, Dad lost his job*
2. *Moved from farm to city*
3. *Turmoil in family*
4. *Memories not clear, feeling of sadness*
5. *See bars of crib? Mother crying, soft light*
6. *Empty feeling, hungry, can't stop crying*

Pace yourself. Begin with several positive stories to build up your writing muscles. When you're ready, dive into a painful story. After writing a painful story, return to the present and nurture yourself, as described in Chapter 7.

Here's another way you can write from your timeline. Randomly choose one of the circles, set a stopwatch or timer for fifteen minutes, and freewrite nonstop about the event named in the chosen circle. Let the words flow, keeping the inner critic at bay. When time is up, choose another circle and write that story for fifteen minutes. Repeat the process for a third circle.

At the end of forty-five minutes you will have the beginnings of three new stories. With these beginnings, you will see how quickly your memoir develops.

Do this intensive work at least once a month.

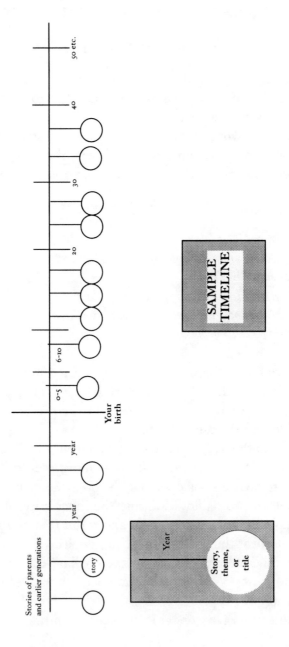

19

Topics and Triggers

I write to discover what I know.
—Flannery O'Connor

emories conjure up people, places, and things that are meaningful and carry energy. Sometimes a sight, smell, or sound can propel us back in time. Such moments can from the past trigger the vignettes and longer stories that will comprise your memoir. It is important to take the time to remember, to meditate on memory and the images we carry for their emotional, visual, and sensual details. We draw upon all this to tell our stories. Note where the emotional "heat" is, what issue or circumstance from the past still stirs up your emotions. It is important to write about those things when they are "hot," as it helps the creative process along. As we write, we learn more about what we think and remember. "It's amazing—the more I write, the more I remember," my students frequently tell me. And it's true.

Your Childhood Home

The house where you grew up or the place where your childhood imagination finds solace lives within you. The placement of closets, windows, and doors; the smells of gardenias and roses, wood smoke and fried chicken; the sounds of creaking floors and windows mark us for life. Thousands of memories of our houses are registered within our very cells as we grow up. Our memories are located there, in that place of early identity, and it is there that we return.

In *The Poetics of Space* Paul Bachelard, the French philosopher, says: "The house we were born in is physically inscribed in us." Bachelard speaks in poetic cadences of the power of childhood spaces, how they define us and enter us, and how we return in dream and reverie to these worlds.

Writing our memories means to enter this childhood dream space. During the first annual Body and Soul Retreat I held in Calistoga, California, I asked students to draw and write about a house that was important to them in their childhood. One person wrote about his grandparents' apartment. We could see how important it was to him as a boy, and how it has become a part of his dream space. Another person wrote about the car that took her and her sister to and from visitations with their parents. The car was the symbol of home, and one of the important spaces that shaped her autobiography.

During my early childhood, my grandmother and I spent most weekends with her best friends, whom I called Aunt Helen and Uncle Maj. In their house on the other side of town, I would find relief from poisonous cigarette smoke and depression. The house had green shingles and red trim, and was surrounded by hundreds of roses. It stood beside Boggy Creek, which flooded so many times that they had to raise the house. In summer the windows were always open; soft breezes carried the scent of roses and sucked the lace curtains in and out of the screens. Aunt Helen's bedroom gave the aroma of her perfumes and powders on her vanity table, and sheets dried in the sun. Every weekend she made delicious homemade bread and soup, Southern fried chicken and gravy.

This was for me the house of comfort and nurturing, love and generosity. Aunt Helen's belly laugh lifted me from worries about my grandmother, giving me hope that happiness and warmth existed in the world.

I still dream of this house, long gone, moved from where it

once reigned over beauty and roses and sweet summer nights. Aunt Helen, Uncle Maj, and the house are alive only inside of me, until I share them with others through my writing.

This poem arose from a dream I had, in half-sleep, about the power and wisdom in old houses.

House of Memory

The house hovers alone in the forest
shrugging off leaves and spores.
It has been in the forest a very long time.

We must be careful—it is replete with memory.
Every plank of wood, painting,
brass fitting has a story to tell.

The house whispers in a language
we do not understand.
It possesses a wisdom
we need to survive.

We sit on couches that
embraced other bodies now vanished,
taking everything they knew with them.

The house knows everything:
how the sun rises, warms kitchen walls.
It has seen the movements of planets, seasons,
how the years unfold like daffodils,
opening, releasing seeds of new life,
withering, dying

The house inhales our dreams,
our words, screams and cries in the night.
Everything is etched in walls,
runes that scramble, scuttle.
You believe it is the sound of mysterious
insects, but it is words trying to be heard.

Who understands the wounds,

the emptiness
when you were flooded with
too much grief

when your child died,
when your parents refused to love you,
when your lover left you for someone else.

The house stands in the woods.
You stand beside it, tilting your head toward
creaking in the wind.
It is empty now, waiting for you to put your
hand on the dusty dented door knob.

Open it carefully
as you would a present
wrapped in gold foil.
Be prepared
to listen.

Nature

When we are children, the world presents itself to us as a place
of wonder and magic. We do not understand the logical world of
adults, and so we turn to the world of nature, which invites us into
its mists and leaves and clouds, scents and rustly grasses, moonlight
and landscapes of beauty. The natural world captures us in its
seasons and rhythms, and reminds us of our own animal wisdom.

  When I was young, the natural world around me was so
powerful it took my breath away—the smell of the air in the
morning, the liquid warmth of summer. Birds calling out from
telephone poles in the middle of the Great Plains lifted my heart.
The dramatic thunderstorms and great panoramas of clouds
made me feel comforted when things were sharp and unpleasant
at home. All I had to do was go outdoors, and the wind would
whisper its comfort to me. The sweeping seas of golden wheat
told me that there was indeed a God who had created such won-
ders. When I was sixteen and wracked with grief over a friend's

suicide, I gathered to my heart comfort from a minuscule violet flower and its fuzzy green leaves. Its natural simplicity calmed my confusion and outrage.

Nature draws us to its eternal cycle of flowering, decaying as the human stories unfold within it. To go deeper into the world of nature, to be uplifted and inspired by mountains, ocean, and forest—these are healing opportunities. We can listen to nature, even take dictation from it, listing its colors and flavors, writing about our sensual experience within its embrace. One of my students, Clare Cooper Marcus, writes extensively in her memoir about this healing aspect of nature. She writes of taking refuge in nature when her family was trying to escape the bombs of London during the war, immersing herself in the scent of loam and the way light played upon the grasses and plants. She says about such a setting, "The troubles of the world disappeared."

Mentors

As Alice Miller has said, when we have compassionate, helping witnesses in our lives, we are given a chance to flower and develop in ways that we might have missed without them. A mentor sees and appreciates us for who we are, and helps us recognize our talents, our creativity, and our real self—the one who shines out in spite of any pain we may be suffering. My mentor was Mr. Brauninger, my cello teacher. The way his blue eyes gazed into mine and his unconditional support helped me survive difficult times with my grandmother. He swept into my life on a fall morning in 1954. He gathered Mrs. Rockwell's fourth grade class into a Pied Piper trance with his violin under his chin, his red hair falling across his forehead, and his smile. I was hooked, and I signed up to play the cello. But more than teaching me how to play the cello, Mr. Brauninger saw the real me.

His hands danced a ballet as he conducted the Youth Symphony each Saturday morning. He introduced the magic of Haydn, Vivaldi, Bach, and Beethoven to us young musicians. He'd sweep us up and excitedly call out, "Give it to me, yes, yes." And the music would gather energy, and we'd rush through millions of notes, half unplayed, stopping breathless at the end, laughing, at one with the music.

I'd do anything to please him, to get that sweet smile to bloom. His blue eyes looked into my soul. With him, I was not just a nothing, an abandoned girl whose parents didn't want her. At symphony, all the shadows were driven away.

He met his future wife, Eva, over the conductor's baton, and all of us in Symphony watched them fall in love. When they left for Washington State where they would be teaching next when I was thirteen, we lost touch for many years. Thirty-five years later, when we were reunited in Des Moines, it seemed like a dream come true. Mr. Brauninger's hair was white, but his blue eyes shone as they always did, and he and Eva both embraced me as if no time had passed.

I asked him how he thought of me when I was a child. He said, "I used to look in your face and see God. I saw God in the eyes of all my young students."

He put a Bach Brandenburg Concerto on his special hi-if and sat facing me in a kind of ecstatic reverie. When our eyes met, we were together again in that wind-blown little town of my childhood.

During his last illness, he held my hand and whispered, "I must have been like a father to you."

Tears formed in my eyes as he spoke what we had never put into words before—my need for a father, the emptiness in my life that Mr. Brauninger had filled. Our eyes locked, and my chest filled with the ache of knowing that I was going to lose him again.

His ability to see the real me had given me something to hold on to. When I hear strains of Beethoven and Bach, Vivaldi and Mozart, I return to the Youth Symphony on a Saturday morning. Mr. Brauninger gathers the music into his hands and releases it. The melodies sweep over me in waves, healing secret wounds.

Photographs

Photographs are a moment of time captured and held in permanent suspension. Do you ever wonder what happened just before a particular photo was taken, or just after? People in motion are caught for a split second, everything they were at that moment locked into the frame forever.

Photographs can be powerful triggers for your own memories; they can stimulate your imagination about ancestors you've never met. In photographs there are hints about a mood, the historical time, customs, and the personalities of the people in the picture.

I invite my therapy clients to bring into sessions casual family photos. I look for clues about the family's closeness, distance, carriage, and demeanor. One woman brought in a snapshot of herself at the age of two, and we spoke about it. Later that week she had a flashback about sexual abuse that changed the course of the therapy. Photos contain powerful messages and clues, if you know how to look for them.

For several years I used photos to uncover the lives of my mother and father. I made a photo etching of my father from birth to death to try to understand his life. I copied photos of him as a young boy on cloth and quilted them—a way for me to be with him, to spend the time with him that we never had while he was alive. Perhaps this was one way of mourning him.

I copied photos of my mother and grandmother, trying to uncover their histories. I wanted to stand in their shoes and see their lives. My first biographies and autobiography took place through art, paintings, and drawings I made from photographs as I searched for answers embedded in those captured moments.

The family photos you inherit are a treasure to be mined. Look deep into the sepia images, the black and white snapshots, and the old Kodak color photos. Look for the hidden stories.

Symbols

Objects in the world carry energy. They are part of our history, speaking to us as silent witnesses. Objects that seem ordinary—a book, a cup, a curtain—are part of our memory tapestry. Some spiritual beliefs hold that all inanimate objects are imbued with energy; all we need to do is tune into them. One such symbol for me is my great-grandmother Blanche's cookstove. It was the hub of the house, where the fire burned in summer and winter, where she cooked, baked, and boiled water for coffee and dishes and sponge baths. The fire was alive; it roared, snapped, and whistled. When it was crackling hot, she'd bake an apple pie. She'd let me roll up newspapers to start the fire, add the kindling. When I want to think of comfort, I think of the stove, how alive it made the kitchen seem and how exciting it was to hear its song and feel its warmth. And most of all, I can still taste the hot cinnamon in those pies.

Some families pass down heirlooms, such as jewelry, furniture, tools, and clothing that are symbols of the past. Often these symbols or objects were gifts from long-loved relatives or friends, and they represent the relationship and its meaning. These symbols may tell a whole story—even the history of the family.

When the pioneers came across the plains they brought with them their most cherished items—tables, crocheted tablecloths, bric-a-brac—that represented the world they left behind. Once they reached rough country, they discovered that they could not continue with their wagons so overloaded. Imagine how difficult it was for them to leave their precious objects along the side of the trail, to let go of the symbols of their old life as they moved toward an uncertain future.

Think about the meaningful objects in your life and what they symbolize to you. Take an inventory of the symbolic objects in your house and how you came to acquire them. They may represent whole stories just waiting for you to discover them.

Main Characters

The people who are the major figures in your life will become the main characters in your memoir. To begin with, write a portrait, a quick verbal sketch of personality, attitude, physical movement, and energy. A portrait gives the reader a sense of the character's beliefs, feelings, traits, sayings, activities, and hobbies; it shows who the person is or was and what he or she meant to you, as well as how he or she looked and sounded.

I used an old photograph of my great-grandfather Lewis, the young man who died a month after he conceived my grandmother in 1894. He looks out of the one photograph I have of him. He was less than twenty-two years old, with large, brown eyes. His hair is shorn, and his lips are full and sensual. His cheekbones, the shape of his face, and those soft eyes mirror back to me my own face and the faces of my mother and grandmother. Lewis's gift to us was his face—it lived on through the generations. I dialogued with him once as I looked at his photograph, talked with him about the generations of our family, the tragedies, and the losses. I told him how he lived in all of us.

Inspired, I went to search for his grave again. My grandmother and Blanche and I had looked for it when I was nine years old. As our shoes sank in the soft grass, Blanche kept muttering, "I know he was buried around here somewhere." We didn't find him that day, but I wanted to find him now.

I looked up the date and place of his death on microfilm in the library and willed myself to find the grave. I drove to the Letts Cemetery and wandered trance-like toward a cedar tree. I turned around—and there he was: Lewis Garrett, the man who had given us his face. All this was inspired by his photograph and my written portrait of him.

Writing about him and to him made him real to me.

Writing Invitations—Main Characters

1. Before writing a portrait of a person, it is important to bring him or her fully to mind. Looking at photographs can help. Another method is to close your eyes and picture the person in his typical environment, doing the usual activities you remember him doing.

2. Write a portrait of someone who will be a main character in your memoir. Remember to use sensual details, including color, scent, sound, and feel. Use metaphors: He looked like Cary Grant. She moved like Marilyn Monroe.

a. Body language How would you describe the person's body movements? Quick, slow, jerky, bulky, sensuous, lilting, blocky? Did a shoulder rise under stress? Did her face wrinkle up in laughter or confusion?

b. The feel, color, and look of emotion. How did the person's face and posture change when sad, angry, joyful, hopeful, disappointed?

3. Now write a story about the person you portrayed.

4. If this person affected or changed your life significantly, write about that.

5. What might your life have been like without this person in it? (Think about the premise in the classic film *It's A Wonderful Life*).

6. Write a portrait of a grandmother, grandfather, or any family member you have never met. Try to imagine him or her living and breathing, walking and talking. If you have a photograph of this person, write about the story behind it.

20

 Themes to Unify Your Stories

Every moment and every event of every man's life on earth plants something in his soul.

—Thomas Merton

nce you have created a series of stories, you may find that they coalesce around one or more themes that run through your life. Some or all of your stories may be linked to such themes as abuse, religion, a mother or father's courage, war, or music. A memoir can be held together by geographic location or landscape or the healing power of animals and trees or a pivotal event. This chapter provides some suggestions about possible themes.

Your memoir's theme will become clear when you answer the question: What is this story about? The why and the how of your story elucidate its meaning. The theme shows the underlining message or a philosophy of life. It is a point of view or lens through which the story is viewed. In his book *Turning Memories into Memoirs*, Denis Ledoux says, "The theme is dependent on your insights."

Turning Points

Many different events can become turning points, moments of change or transformation, in our lives: meeting someone for the first time, spiritual experiences, joyous events such as birth and marriage, and traumatic events such as the death of someone important to us. Turning points can be seen as wholly positive or as a mixture of positive and negative. A turning point shakes us up and makes us see life through a different lens. It's a time of power and energy, a doorway into the next chapter of our lives. Here are some important turning points to consider.

Illness: An illness or accident has the potential to change our lives forever. When we become physically or mentally ill, our world is suddenly, irrevocably changed. Illness forces us to reorder what is most important to us. It reminds us of the fragility of life, and the limitations of the body and mind. Having a serious illness can be like traveling through a dark, disordered world where we don't know the landmarks and every step is frightening. Medical memoirs, like *Immune Dysfunction: Winning My Battle Against Toxins, Illness & the Medical Establishment,* by Judith Lopez, focus on such experiences. In his book *A Whole New Life,* Reynolds Price writes about his spinal cancer and paralysis, coming to terms with the spiritual in his life, and how to have hope when there seems to be nothing to hope for. There is a whole genre of memoirs about illness and recovery. These true stories help those who are confronted with similar traumatic experiences to learn how to keeping going, to survive and cope with events that at first seem to be without hope or the potential for growth.

Even a brief illness like the flu forces us to rest and heal our bodies. This shift in our regular routine can give us the needed perspective to re-assess our lives. Illness can be a great teacher, a painful experience that brings up ancient forgotten wounds. Writing our way through it helps us center ourselves anew as we give voice to our fears, hopes, pain, and frustration. In our journals we capture the daily story, and in our memoir, we track the arc of the experience, from diagnosis to treatment and recovery.

Illness can become a metaphor for the journey through life, and our ability to find ourselves and our center as we pass through its stages. As in the hero's journey, we encounter dark forests, wraiths, and frightening monsters; but guides come to help us, and unexpected witnesses assist us along the way.

Death and Loss: One of the most emotionally wrenching turning points in our lives is the death of someone we love. The death of a person, or even a pet who is close to us, creates a permanent change and a heartrending sense of loss. We know that life will never be the same.

Whether the death is preceded by a long, painful illness or is sudden and unexpected, the effect is devastating and traumatic. The people we love are woven throughout the tapestry of our lives and our identity. Letting go of them means letting go of a part of ourselves. Recovering from loss happens in stages—shock, anger, sadness, and layers of emotions. After a long illness and vigil, the actual death can feel like a relief, which in turn can create guilt. And regardless of the circumstances, death can cause depression in the survivors.

Writing has been proven to help resolve depression. Because the same symptoms—tiredness, lethargy, a sense of hopelessness and helplessness—accompany both depression and mourning, writing will no doubt help mourners as well. Journal writing in particular can be useful in recording the changes and feelings that accompany loss.

Many stories can be told about the dying process, from the beginning diagnosis through treatment and the progression toward death. During that process, new relationships are forged and old ones let go of. Sometimes needed resolutions to problems happen during the dying process. It is a time of potential healing for all, but the healing does not always occur. The old patterns may persist, and the family must come to terms with that, as well. The shared stories of the family provide a powerful way to learn to let go.

As you write, memories may come in rapid flashbacks of shared events. It may be painful to write down the exact details about your loved one or about the dying process you witnessed. The natural release of feelings during this kind of writing helps to heal a bruised and aching heart and shepherds you into the next stage of your own life.

And it is not only a recent death that we may want to process through writing. Years after the death of someone close to us, we may find ourselves mourning, feeling unresolved or with questions about their death and our feelings about it. It helps to journal or to write stories about those with whom we have shared our time on the earth, and find a way to say good-bye.

Birth: A baby comes into the world and into his family in the middle of a story in progress. His arrival creates a turning point for everyone, changes the family, and forges new relationships in the community. Each child figures out his role in the family and his place in the community, and eventually learns the stories that he is part of. The birth of any child into a family and community sends roots and shoots in all directions, from childcare workers to neighbors, teachers, and anyone else the child comes in contact with.

When we create new life, our own lives are changed forever. Most of us look into the baby's eyes and see ourselves as we imagine a happy future together. The birth of a child is most often a joyous event. But in some families a child may be unwelcome because it puts a burden on finances. There might be questions about parentage. And in some cases there is the question of whether to keep the baby or give it up for adoption, a difficult issue to resolve.

Because birth occurs in the context of community and family, birth practices (home or hospital delivery, doctor, nurse, midwife, doula) are part of every birth story. To write the story of your own birth, you need to know how you came into the world and what birthing traditions accompanied your entrance. Perhaps you already know about your birth from family stories or other sources.

When I was grown, my grandmother's best friend told me that my grandmother had not wanted to take on that role. She was a young 51 and was irritated to hear that her "youthful" identity had changed. She threw down the telegram that announced my arrival and said, "So, the little brat is born." It would have been hard to guess then that she would start raising me herself when I was five. But the pattern of being an unwilling grandmother continued in her daughter, my mother. She saw each of my three children only twice in their lives, for an hour each time. She raged against being a grandmother and refused to participate. I understood that something was wrong with her, but it was painful to have her reject not only me, but also my children.

Our society equates birth with happiness and normalcy, but many families don't live up to this expectation of society, and their birth stories stay buried out of shame and pain. No one wants to hear about a mother who rejected her children; no one wants to know about this dark side of human nature. But for the family members, these stories cause wounds that are hard to heal, and they must be told to help release the grip they have on the soul. Birth stories range from those of beauty and great love to those of rejection and pain. Think about how you want to tell your story.

Give yourself permission to write about your journey through one or more major turning points in your life. You can be a compassionate witness to your own story.

Writing Invitations—Turning Points

1. List the various positive and negative turning points in your life.

2. Choose one turning point and write a story describing the event, the people involved, your immediate and long-lasting reaction to it, and how your life would have been different if the event had not happened.

3. Write about a time when you were sick as a child or as an adult. How did your body feel? How did your family deal with your illness?

4. If you have had a serious illness, consider writing about your life before, during, and after it occurred. In terms of your healing, what did you hope for? What disappointments did you have? What were the positive aspects of your illness? What have you learned because of it? How has it changed you?

5. Choose a loved person or pet who died or a loved object that you lost. Write about the first time you met, describing your thoughts and feelings about the relationship at the time. Write a character sketch of a loved person who died, describing him at several different moments in time,

including turning points in your relationship. Write about how your life would have been different without this person.

6. Describe how you were changed by the person's life and death.

7. Write the stories you know about your own birth. Include information about how you learned these stories. If you know about birth practices during your mother's or grandmother's generation, write about them also.

8. If you are a father, write about your child's birth, how you got to know your child, how the experience of fatherhood differed or was the same as you thought it would be, and how life changed after the child's arrival.

9. If you are a woman, write about how you came to know about conception and the birth process.

10. If you are a mother, write about your pregnancies and deliveries, and the similarities or differences between them. Describe the story that was already in progress when each of your children was born.

Rituals

Rituals are a way of saying hello and good-bye, announcing intentions, and making changes. Rituals mark a transition from one state to another—a state of consciousness or shift in identity. Public holidays, such as Thanksgiving, take on ritual status, as do graduations and private holidays, such as birthdays or anniversaries. Cooking and feasting can be a big part of celebrations, and food is an important aspect of family life. Whole memoirs can be written about food, such as *Tender at the Bone: Growing Up at the Table* by Ruth Reichl.

Rituals are at the heart of most religious celebrations. When Hitler wanted to deny the identity and rights of the Jewish people, he took away their ability to celebrate holy days by forbidding the purchase of wine, matzo, and ritual food for Passover. Food is often used for comfort; food rituals soothe family dynamics. When the weekly homemade bread or cake or pot roast is missing, that means something is wrong in the family.

Rituals may be as simple as lighting candles, watering plants, brushing the cat. Walking a dog twice a day can be a pleasant ritual that helps release the cares of the day. Meditation and yearly vacations, revisiting beautiful landscapes such as Yosemite or the desert can all become rituals. Vision quests and retreats are a part of renewal rituals for many people, in which a part of the self is let go and another part is invited forward. A ceremony such as a christening, bris, baptism, bar mitzvah, and marriage is a way to ritualize progress through life's stages. Many modern rituals derive from ancient pagan ceremonies; some are even celebrated today, such as midsummer at Stonehenge.

Writing Invitations—Rituals

1. Write about your favorite ritual, or one that is unique to your family, or the one you most closely identify with your family.

2. Describe any rituals that you don't like or that make you feel uncomfortable or angry.

3. Write about the family rituals you hope your children will continue to observe after they leave home. Why do those rituals have special significance for you?

Love and Friendship

Our lives are woven through with love stories—romantic love, friendship, love of family, love of pets. Students in my memoir classes frequently tell their stories of first love. This story of awakening takes us past the threshold of family love and into the larger world.

Most people have a special place in their hearts for first love. We always remember the first time our pulse raced at the sight of someone who made the world look brighter and better. A first love shines in our mind forever, like a bright star, imbued with the yearning and dreams of our younger selves.

Mature or maturing love is like good wine that needs time to bloom into its fullest flavor. As we mature, we come to understand that feelings, emotions, and attachments rise and fall like the seasons. Whole books are written about one relationship, how it began, how it progressed through peaks and valleys, and how love bursts out of its boundaries in surprising ways. You might write such a memoir.

Writing about our best friends or the friendships we have had in our lives makes us remember the joy of discovery, of getting to know a person, letting go of expectations and clichés, sharing and laughing and crying together during upheavals and triumphs. Friends help us figure out who we are, and offer their love and witnessing. As you consider love and friendship in your life, think about the time you first realized the importance of friends, and think about what kind of friend you are to others.

The old phrase "blood is thicker than water" carries considerable weight in our culture. But some people don't have blood relations they can count on; instead, they discover that their friends are their "real" family. Many people come from fractured families and homes in which abuse, violence, and lack of safety dominate. When homes are unsafe, young people go out into the world to find comfort, protection, and a new identity. Each year thousands of abused children run away to a new "family" on the street. Through the years, abused children who have survived into adulthood have searched for and found family in new friends, often "adopting" them and being adopted into the newfound family.

Anais Nin says, "Each friend represents a world in us, a world possibly not born until they arrive, and it is only by this meeting that a new world is born."

Writing Invitations—Love and Friendship

1. Describe meeting your first love. Include sensual details and show how you felt during and after this first meeting.

2. If your first love was also your first dating or sexual experience, write about how you think this has affected your ongoing romantic relationships.

3. Explain what you have learned about maturing love and how a maturing love relationship has shifted your philosophy of life, or given you new strengths or boundaries.

4. Make a list of your friends, telling when and how you met, and why you became friends.

5. Choose a best friend or lover and write about how he or she has changed your life.

Sexuality

Sex is part of our lives, a part of being embodied and being creative human beings, but sex is often not written into a life story. Sex may be a joyous part of our lives or a part of our pain and sorrow, but it is almost always significant. Each person has a sexual history that informs choices, feelings, and decisions. Sex can cause a great deal of confusion and pain; sometimes it is fraught with shame and guilt.

We learn about sexuality from a number of different sources—from friends, family, and society. Silence on the subject can teach us it is wrong to have sexual feelings, or that we are wrong or bad. Religion often teaches that sex is bad and shameful. Such lessons burn into the psyche, creating a wound that is difficult to heal. Sex is full of energy and danger—it can be ecstatic and fulfilling, or it can draw us into darkness.

As we grow and develop, our true sexual feelings and identity may be a secret, even from ourselves. We may learn from unspoken rules as well as cruel jokes and ridicule that we must hide the truth, from ourselves as well as from others.

Writing about our sexuality tunes us in to the power in saying what is true—our honest and real feelings and experiences. Using words to tell our true stories about sex, writing about the negative experiences along with the happy, joyous experiences, gives us a sense of empowerment. Most of us have been taught to use euphemisms about sex, but it is important, when writing to heal, that we give ourselves permission to use all the words, both slang and correct medical terms, to describe our experience.

Unfortunately, many stories about sex are about sexual abuse. The abused person feels shame and guilt. Writing about it can cause great psychic pain and bring the trauma back. If you have suffered sexual abuse and want to write, be sure that you have the support of a therapist or good friend. You might try writing around the incident first rather than writing about it directly. (For more about writing around a painful subject, see Chapter 4.)

Writing Invitations—Sexuality

1. In your private journal, list any secret sex stories you've never told or written about.

2. Write about how and from whom you learned about sex as a child, whether by example or with words, and tell how you felt about sex then.

3. Describe your first sexual experience, remembering to include sensory details.

4. If one or more particular sexual experience changed the direction of your life, for better or worse, write about that.

5. Describe how you have felt about your sexuality throughout your life and how your sexuality has changed over the years.

Spirituality

Another possible theme for a memoir is your spiritual development, your struggle to find a religion, a religious calling, or God. A spiritual autobiography is a story of healing; uniting soul and body, and finding a deeper meaning that gives comfort and solace, direction and intention.

Thomas Merton writes of his journey to become a priest in his spiritual autobiography *The Seven Storey Mountain*. He begins with his birth in France and talks about how he wrestled with different forces in himself and in his life to find his way to Gesthemane, a Trappist monastery in Kentucky, where he became a monk. His search for God is lyrical and passionate, later tempered by his exposure to other religions, including Buddhism. He was a prolific poet and wrote many books about his lifelong spiritual search.

In my Spiritual Autobiography class I ask students to trace their development through pain, darkness, and suffering, from the lost self or false self into transformational moments that have freed them.

The word "spirituality" comes from the Latin root "spirare," which means to breathe. We have imbued it with the meaning of breathing in or taking in God, a higher power, or an energy force that guides the universe. There is no one right way to view this force; every religion and spiritual path has its own way of defining and experiencing it. People find guidance in different ways—some through meditation and prayer, some through solitude in nature; some gradually, and others through an epiphany.

Some writers include stories about their childhood spirituality in their memoirs. If religion or spirituality played an important role in your childhood, you might want to do the same, including stories about how you first experienced God or had a sense of being a part of something larger than yourself. Include what your understanding of religion made you think about yourself as a person, and how you came to terms with any contradictions you may have encountered.

In his book *The Story of Your Life: Writing a Spiritual Autobiography*, Dan Wakefield says that we are changed by writing from a holistic or spiritual perspective and come to understand ourselves in a new way. "By remembering and writing down our past from a spiritual perspective . . . we can sometimes see and understand it in a way that makes it different."

A spiritual autobiography invites you to write from the heart and to explore the parts of yourself and your inner voice that you might censor or that are too vulnerable and private to announce to the world. It is the story of becoming on the deepest level, the story of your soul's journey.

Writing Invitations—Spirituality

1. Write about your spiritual philosophy and what the word "soul" means to you.

2. Describe when and how you began to suspect that spirituality might not be the same as religion and tell your thoughts about the differences.

3. Write about what religions or spiritual paths you have explored, what you have learned, and how you apply this knowledge to your life.

4. Describe your current spiritual life and the elements it may include, such as meditation, prayer, sacred readings, religion, church, or other kinds of worship.

21

 ## Using the Techniques of Fiction

Whatever you can do or dream you can, begin it.
Boldness has genius, power and magic in it.
Begin it now.

—Goethe

emoirs written for today's audiences read like fiction, with scenes, characters, dialogue, and description. The goal of fiction is to create a believable world, a fictive dream that a reader can enter and linger in without waking up until the dream ends. Tristine Rainer calls this style of memoir writing the "new autobiography." In her book *Your Life as Story: Discovering the "New Autobiography" and Writing Memoir as Literature*, Rainer traces the history of memoir and autobiography. Autobiography has always been social history; it used to be written in essay style, without scenes or other fictional devices.

Instead of being written only by the famous, many published memoirs today are written by ordinary people. The reading public has discovered that anyone can have an interesting life. Readers dive into a memoir eager for a story of how real people lived. Rainer says, "The new autobiography, having moved into the literary arena of poetry and fiction, is now concerned with the larger truths of myth and story."

Your memoir will "sing" as you develop your writing skills and become adept at using writing tools found in good fiction. To make your story come alive, you must let readers see the characters in action. Readers identify with the protagonist, the narrator of the story, which is you, and they see through your eyes.

Description provides visual cues for the scene. Sensual details, such as smell, sound, taste, and texture, bring the fictive world alive and make readers feel the scene in their bodies and minds. Those details make readers live in a story and keep them connected to it. Dialogue gives the characters voice and personality as they act and react. Conflict and plot make readers eager to see what happens next and create a sense of forward motion in your story.

Scene, Summary, and Reflection

In a memoir, events are presented in three ways: in a scene, in a summary, and in a reflection. An author's reflections about her story distinguish a memoir from fiction. A scene, through narrative, dialogue, and exposition of details, shows the action in real time, delineates characters, and reveals plot. Description lets the reader *see* the place and the action; *hear* the sound of the environment—nature, wind, household activities; and *experience* the feel of clothes on skin, the humidity, the sun, or the dampness of fog.

Scene

Include these eight elements in your scenes:

1. **Setting:** Where does this moment of action takes place?
2. **Characters:** Who is on stage interacting and showing who they are?
3. **Context:** What is going on emotionally? What is the point of the scene?
4. **Action:** How do people move; what are they doing?
5. **Dialogue:** Do you use dialogue to show character and point of view?
6. **Conflict:** How do you show that each character has a desire, and that these desires present conflicting aspects of plot?

7. Historical time: During what historical time does the story take place?

8. Sensual details: How do you use descriptions to show how things feel, sound, look, taste, and smell to bring people and times alive on the page?

Summary

A summary gives an overview of the scene, compressing it into a few lines. It may include reflection as well as a literal summing up of the action, the context, and how time has passed. Several years can be summarized in a sentence: "For the next five years they lived on the farm. Then one day . . ."

Reflection

Memoirs also contain reflection—the private thoughts of the narrator's inner self, a musing, retrospective voice. In this voice the narrator becomes philosophical and questioning, searching for understanding and perspective. Reflections are one of the healing aspects of memoir writing.

The following scene, summary, and reflection are from my autobiography. In the scene, notice the use of sensual detail and description, some dialogue, and a specific sense of place and time.

Scene: The heat of the July day rises up from the land. Everything smells like fresh air and earth. The tomatoes are ripening, round globules of green, yellow, and red hanging pendulous from the vines. Blanche snaps off a tomato and bites into it. Juice runs down the crevices of her chin. Her deep-set, wise eyes, behind gold-rimmed spectacles, gaze at me.

"Mmm," she mutters, gesturing that I should pick one. I hesitate. Everything is too raw, too close to the earth. I am awe-stricken and a little frightened. Bugs and dirt are everywhere. Flies buzz and ants crawl. Gnats fly in my mouth and stick in the corners of my eyes. Blanche gestures at the tomatoes, and I pluck one with a satisfying snap. Everything smells of tomato—acrid and a little bitter. The skin doesn't give in to my teeth. I feel silly. Blanche is a pioneer woman,

born in 1873, and she tells me to eat it.

"Come on, bite down hard."

"But it's dirty."

"You got to eat a peck o' dirt 'fore you die. Come on." She smears yellow seeds around on her chin with her sleeve. She seems unsophisticated and rough, but I feel guilty of having that thought.

"Come on. Try it. It's good for ya. Nothin' like the fruit of the earth."

My teeth pierce the skin; juices flood my mouth and run down my throat. I choke, flooded with tomato, the sun on my head, the smell of earth. Her eyes laugh behind her glasses; her mouth curls up a little.

"Good, ain't it?" she says and turns around to savagely hoe the weeds that try to take away her vegetables.

The life of the land belongs to Blanche, just as it did to the Native Americans who planted corn on this very spot. Blanche sucks in air, spits out a few seeds. They will take root next year, nurtured by soil and sun, and the deep-rooted water under the land, the Mississippi sending out its life-giving waters, part of the endless cycle of life.

Summary: The day we arrived in Iowa, my great-grandmother Blanche took me out to the garden to help her hoe weeds. She insisted that I eat a ripe tomato, and she told me about our family. That whole summer when I was seven, and all the summers of my childhood, I would learn about Blanche's history and how a pioneer woman managed to live in the 1900s.

Reflection: When I think back to those days, I realize it was then that I began to be the family historian. I absorbed those nights in the featherbed, the wood cookstove, the sepia family pictures, the hints and snapshots of the past. The past seemed more alive than the present. History was a silent ghost beside me as I walked through the garden or peered at moss-covered stones in the cemetery. Later, in my forties and fifties, when my cousin took out the old box of photographs, I would be transported back to being a little girl looking into the faces of the old ones beside me and their youthful counterparts in the picture, seeing what was in store for me.

Point of View

You, the writer, have two roles. You are the *narrator* of the story and a main character, all at once. The *first person* point of view is through the eyes of the "I" character. Every member of the family has his or her own point of view, but because you lead the reader through your eyes, you have the last word.

Singular	**Plural**
First person: I	First person: we
Second person: you	Second person: you
Third person: he, she	Third person: they

Tone

The narrator's tone conveys subtleties, music that comes through in the text. Tone, also referred to as voice, shows mood and attitude; it can be serious or playful, intimate or reserved, cheerful or somber. It can also be angry or loving, subtle or blunt, casual or high-toned, commanding or submissive. Tone is shown through cadence and word choice. Words may be poetic or practical, hard-edged or soft. Hard words convey conflict or bleakness: cut, slashed, steel, doom, gray. Soft words convey vulnerability or kindness: whisper, murmur, sing, caress, longing.

Tell a story into a tape recorder, and listen to your own voice. Then listen to a friend's voice. To understand tone or voice, observe speech patterns around you, eavesdrop in malls and coffee shops. Listen to the way people speak, how they use words. As you read, be aware of voice; notice the way a narrator draws you in, or fails to. Think about the kinds of words, images, and moods that appeal to you.

Dialogue

Dialogue is often one of the more challenging fiction techniques. It takes time to learn how to capture people's speech patterns and make them sound natural. Dialogue reveals a character's attitude, feelings, background, and level of education. It also reveals place—

through accent, word usage or dialect, and cadence. Dialogue needs to be natural, yet it isn't an exact translation of how people actually talk. When you write dialogue you don't include all the hesitations and errors that occur in spoken language.

Quotation marks frame direct dialogue, and, in American English, the end punctuation goes inside the mark:

She said, "I'm leaving, I tell you, and you can't stop me."

When you need to indicate which character spoke the dialogue, it's best to use the conventional verb "said":

"Please, please, don't go. I'll do anything," he said.

Verbs that show emotion, such as "pleaded" or "whined" or "screamed," can detract from the dialogue. Instead of *telling* readers how the characters feel, let the characters' words *show* their emotion.

Too much direct dialogue can cause time to slow down in a scene. Too much back and forth feels like a tennis match. For variety, use indirect dialogue:

She told me she was going to leave me. She said she never wanted to see me again, and she sat back in her seat, sipping her tea.

But direct dialogue is often the most effective way to move a story along.

Most students come to me afraid to write direct dialogue. Like other writing skills, it takes practice. When I first started writing, I used no dialogue at all, but I practiced while sitting in cafés, taking dictation from those around me as I tried to learn how to write the way people spoke. I edited out the umms and ahhs so typical in regular speech. I practiced writing the different ways that people speak.

Practice. Listen to those around you. Sharpen your ear. Read dialogue written by others and keep writing it yourself until it becomes a natural part of your writing toolbox.

Setting, Landscape, and Place

As a child, I lived on the Great Plains of Oklahoma. The land went on forever. I grew up under a huge blue canopy of sky; against the blue was an ever moving panorama of clouds, huge white towers that seemed to rise up to heaven and morphed into fantastic shapes.

Weather was always on our minds. It ruled the plains with tempestuous storms and great shows of flickering lightning. Gathering storms made the sky go pea green and a sick purple. We were always on the watch for tornadoes. We listened for tornado warnings and sirens, and prepared our houses and ourselves for the terrible thing that might sweep down out of the sky and destroy us.

There was a terrifying beauty in it all, and a thrill that coursed through my body when thunder-and-lighting storms struck. The wind tore at the house and tugged and tugged as if in the next gust it would rip it apart. The weather-stripping in the windows and doors sang like a kazoo as the wind forced its way in. The chorus of kazoo, thunder rumbles, and crashes of the wind made for a raucous summer afternoon.

Setting and place shape people and affect their lives profoundly. The location creates situations that people must react to, events that become part of their story. Every setting in the world has its own unique character, people and animals, vegetation and weather. When you write your story, think about how the weather, the landscape—mountain, beach, desert, forest—the nation and culture have affected the people you write about. Make your characters act and react in this setting.

If you do not know much about a setting where your characters are depicted, conduct research. To give a place and time verisimilitude, you need to be authentic. Some memoirs are highly researched, with dates, times, newspaper articles, and facts woven throughout as a way to guard against too much subjectivity. Geological history, weather events, disasters such as blizzards, floods, earthquakes, and dust storms all have an impact on the history of a place and a people.

Setting influences characterization: how people interact, what they do day-to-day, their attitudes, dress, meals, events. For example, a person on a farm gets up early, feeds the animals, and carries responsibility for many other living beings; she may wear dungarees and eat her main meal in the middle of the day. An urban setting presents a different mood, lifestyle, and set of problems. Opportunities, routines, and duties differ depending on place. Life in a ghetto is different from life in a middle-class multicultural neighborhood or a palatial estate.

A setting in a foreign city will be unique to that place, and the description of it must reflect the flavor and taste and mood of the city at that time. The names of streets, cafés, and famous buildings can paint the picture. No city is like any other. Describe with accurate details the buildings, land, and colors, the movement, mood, and feeling in the town.

Setting determines atmosphere and mood. Think about how each of the following settings creates a different emotional sense:

• A crowded, bustling street
• A beach in moonlight
• A rundown rooming house
• A New York subway at night
• The desert in August

What pictures form in your mind when you think of these places? What kind of mood does each one suggest? Poetic? Gritty? Different feelings arise when thinking of different landscapes. One thing you can do is to write character portraits of different landscapes, the feelings they evoke in you, and your response to them. The way you feel about the setting will help determine your tone and the mood you convey in your writing through choice of language.

Structure and Time

Because memoir explores life over time, as a memoir writer you will enter different life histories at different times in their development. There are various ways to structure your memoir and to move back and forth in time. The timeline, described in Chapter 18, helps you keep track of the time frame for a particular scene or story.

Presenting your stories in chronological order is one way to structure your book. Or you might decide to build the structure around characters, devoting a separate chapter or section of your book to each character and following him or her through time. You might also choose to intersperse sections of present time reflections with chapters about the past that carry the voice or tone of the past.

Tense

You can use different verb tenses to move around in time:

Present tense refers to current time: *I drive.*

Present progressive tense refers to ongoing current action: *I am driving.*

Past tense refers to the recent past: *I drove.*

Past perfect tense refers to an action beyond the recent past: *I had driven.*

So a memoirist writing from the point of view of her seven-year-old self might say:

> I *wish* I had a puppy dog. Of course I *am wishing* for any kind of pet. Last year I *wished* for a kitten, but then I changed my mind. Before that, when I was really little, I *had wished* for a goldfish.

If you are confused about using verb tenses to move through time, it will help to pay particular attention to tense in your reading and to practice using the different tenses in your own writing.

Flashback:

One way to look at the past is through flashbacks. Flashbacks work the way memory works. Let's say I return to Iowa in the summer. I am standing in the garden as an adult, and suddenly I see and hear events that happened forty years ago. I am living a flashback at that moment. When writing flashbacks, you need to give your readers clues that you are moving from one time to another by choosing appropriate verb tenses.

You can structure your flashbacks in two ways, taking care to be consistent as you go back and forth between time frames:

1. Begin in the *present,* using present tense. *Flash back to the past,* using *past tense.* Return to the present, using the present tense and end in the present tense. You can insert a blank line to indicate a break between time frames.

> *I look at the photograph of my mother, her dark hair curled around her face, her dark eyes soft. Then I see her the way she was that day as she appeared at the front door, a surprise.*
>
> *I was nine years old, and as I always did each Saturday afternoon, I was practicing the piano. There was a knock on the door, and when I opened it, all the blood seemed to drain into my feet. An apparition of my mother stood there, a slight smile on her face. I knew she was real when I heard her voice.*
>
> *I whisper to her now, an ache in my chest . . .*

2. Begin in the *past tense* but in *present time* frame. Flash back into the *past* in the *present tense.* This technique of using present tense for the past brings the reader directly into the past as if it is happening now, thus making it more intense. End in the *past tense* located in *present time.*

> *I flipped through the dusty courthouse records, looking for the name of my grandmother when she was twenty years old, the year her baby boy was stillborn.*
>
> *I see her pacing up and down the living room of the small apartment. The pains are coming stronger now; she bends down and catches her side. One long breath after the other as the wind forces bits of ice between the edges of the windowpane . . .*

The child's name was Harrison Hawkins, written in graceful cursive, the birth and death, the same day: January 14, 1929.

Writing Invitations

1. Practice dialogue by choosing two characters in your story; freewrite a conversation in which they disagree. Write the same conversation in indirect dialogue. Which is better?

2. Using sensual details, describe a major setting or landscape, a town, village, or city that is important in your story.

3. Start a story in the present. Flash back to the past using a link between then and now such as an object or a detail—the weather, the smell of coffee—linking the time frames. End in present time.

4. Write a significant scene that occurred when you were ten years old. Make sure we know who, what, where, and when in the scene. Use dialogue to show character, and sensual details to bring the scene alive.

5. Write a summary version of that scene. Compare the two.

22

Researching the Hidden Stories

The voyage of discovery lies not in finding new landscapes but in having new eyes.

— Marcel Proust

Ill my life I was intensely curious about the past. I loved hearing stories about earlier generations in my family that wove through conversations at the dinner table in Iowa. Every summer for forty years, more than a dozen of my grandmother's brothers and sisters, with their husbands and wives would gather for fried chicken dinner, my aunts in their homemade aprons decorated with rickrack and tied over generous bellies, the men's voices deep as they discussed the weather, the hayin' season, coon hunting.

The formica table would be fitted with extra leaves, and for birthdays and Christmas they'd use the good china and "silver"—actually stainless steel—set on freshly ironed tablecloths laid end to end. The stories made their way around the table, the volume rising when one person remembered an event differently than another. After corn on the cob, mashed potatoes, and gravy scraped clean from the electric skillet, the sun would begin its slow golden glow as it set behind Eisely Hill.

The men retired to lawn chairs outside to light their pipes and talk, while my aunts flicked each other with dishtowels, whispering dirty jokes out of the corners of their mouths, their faces bright from the hot soapy water and the fun of breaking the rules—women should never talk dirty, women should always have clean minds and houses.

After the dishes were washed and put away, the smell of perked coffee filled the house. Chocolate cake with chocolate frosting and peach and lemon meringue pies that I had helped create were served on dessert dishes. Around the table they all returned, and the long, slow stories would unwind. "Remember when . . . Who's Uncle Lem . . . What part of the family did they come from . . . Don't you remember the house that Edith was born in . . . the old peach orchard . . . the smoke house . . ."

Aunt Edith would bring out the box of black-and-white photos. All their stories had illustrations: model T's, horses and wagons, barns, and old-fashioned clothes. They looked jaunty and young and hopeful as they stared at the camera, and around the table I could feel a wistfulness for "the old days."

I learned about the culture of a family whose history was written in the graveyards for fifty miles around. Since 1850 the family had farmed the land and raised children, and that's what life was all about—making sure no one went hungry, being proud of independence no matter how many of the family myths were untrue or how much false pride may have filled the room.

The numbers around the table dwindled as these relatives died one by one. I was left to make sense of this family that I was a part of and yet wasn't. Because my grandmother had a different father than her siblings, she wasn't a full blood relation. Because she had left her daughter behind and flaunted her riches, she was "other," and so would I be one day because I was not part of the folks who stayed near the land, near the birthplaces.

But their history is my history, and I became even more curious about it.

The history of the land and the family clung to me like the fog of the Mississippi River bottom. I imagined that I could see moccasin tracks of the Indians on the riverbank, now protected by a high levee. The most important river in the United States seemed to belong to us, to me. The river and its history and spirit had woven through the "blood dream" of our generations like a spiritual father.

As an adult I followed up these imaginings by doing research about the land and our family's history. I wanted to know the Indian tribes who had harvested the land before the whites came. Blanche had told me about the Indians who came to the farms looking for food. I discovered that the land had belonged to the Sac and the Fox tribes, and that the town of Muscatine got its name from Mouscatin, another tribe of Indians from that area. Wapello, the town where my mother had been born, was named for Chief Wapello, one of Black Hawk's chiefs. Black Hawk was forced to make peace with the whites in 1837. My childhood imaginings were not that far off. Maybe the spirits of the Native Americans really were embedded in the land; maybe their spirits still roamed the banks of the Mississippi River as I'd imagined.

Questions about my mother and grandmother led me to dusty county courthouses in small towns and the microfilm archives of newspapers, including the newspaper owned by my maternal grandfather's family, *The Wapello Republican*. For ten years I examined yellowed certificates of birth, marriage, and death to mine the when and where, and who.

It was exciting to find the original signatures of Blanche and her husband Lewis on their wedding certificate. I had few clues about my mother and her childhood, but I felt as if I was bringing my mother's childhood back to her, knitting the broken threads of the past as I did my research. My great-aunts and -uncles seemed to have no answers about my mother's past or didn't want to talk about some of the shameful stories that had trickled through the family folklore. I was upsetting the applecart by asking all kinds of nosy questions. "The past is the past, and it should stay in the past," they'd say, tight-lipped as they looked away.

The Imagined Story

Research often produces more speculation than facts. But research can fill in your imagination and give you ideas about the way lives were lived, and it may help you write a story about a relative you've never met. Writing the imagined story is a way to fill in the blanks of missed history and story, and it helps our healing process. Our imaginings might be closer to the truth than we would have guessed.

One of my students, Sarah Weinberg, (see page 222) had always been curious about her great-grandfather, a man whose name was not even known. In her mind she began to hear the cadences of his speech and imagine his life. Research on the Internet gave her information about the town he might have come from, the customs of the town, and what it might have been that caused him to send his children to America yet not arrive there himself. No one in the family knew what had happened to him, but all this new information gave her a way to enter his story through her imagination.

Information Sources

Your research may involve as little as asking family members for information or as involved as sending for public records or visiting old neighborhoods and towns to find original documents and stories.

Information about marriages, deaths, and births can be found on genealogical sites on the Internet, and you can research military records, the census, and professions online. Newspapers and libraries have researchable archives online as well, but some records must be found at the source, which means a research trip to the town or county where they are located. Some of my students have discovered long-hidden facts about psychiatric hospitalization; others have unearthed family stories that have been kept secret for decades, buried in lies and cover-ups because of shame.

When I decided to write the imagined story of my grandmother's elopement in 1911 and the birth of her stillborn son a year before my mother's birth, I researched the town and how life was lived at the time—the kind of clothes worn, how houses were kept warm, the presence or absence of electricity, telephone, and indoor plumbing. In my imagined scenario, this stillbirth took place in winter during a snowstorm that delayed the doctor. Later, when I found the child's birth and death certificates, I found that they did indeed occur in winter, January 29, 1914. His death resulted from prolonged labor, during which the cord wrapped around his neck. The story I imagined was amazingly similar to the actual events.

I read books and stories written by local residents, reminiscences and memoirs about life during different eras in that place. Other useful resources included Sears and Montgomery Ward catalogues, which showed the kinds of goods that people used at the time, giving me authentic details.

Old photos, letters, family bibles, journals and diaries, attic trunks, old books, keys, tools, recipes—all these family items can give you clues to the stories you seek. Libraries collect local histories, biographies, and memoirs; such stories also appear online. From phone books you can put together the history of where a family member lived and worked. I found my father listed in the Louisville phone book: it gave his address and his employment. Going through several phone books, I traced his whereabouts in the decades before I was born, which helped make his life real to me thirty years after his death.

Interviews with relatives may be audio- or videotaped. Genealogists combine those tapes with written stories that provide an archive for storytellers like you.

Weaving the imagined story with facts and accurate details can be healing. By creating a story, the writer heals the torn fragments of family life as she fills in the unknown, empty places. Writing the imagined story of the stillbirth of my grandmother's first child gave me compassion for her as a young girl of twenty and helped me let go of some of the anger I felt toward her.

Research Steps

As you write your first draft, keep track of the details that need to be researched. Descriptions of clothes, hairstyles, household appliances, cars, houses, and neighborhoods all need to be accurate to create verisimilitude. In between sessions of actual writing, you can do the research.

• Examine photos for details that you can use in your stories.
• Interview family, neighbors, and community members for stories, details, and history.
• Use public resources such as libraries, newspapers, and court records to trace your family's history and immigration background.

Once you have gathered all the details, you can complete an imagined story of an unknown ancestor or a family member you knew but want to understand better.

Writing Invitations

1. Make a list of the relatives you might interview to find out more about your personal history. Make an appointment to make an audio recording of a conversation if you can.

2. Search your family name on the genealogical Internet sites.

3. Go through old photos, looking for clues to the times in which your relatives lived. Write a story from the point of view of one of your ancestors in his or her point of view, using "I."

4. Search newspaper microfilms in the towns where your relatives lived for articles about them. Make copies, and use them as a basis for stories.

5. Look up family births, deaths, and marriages in courthouse archives. How does seeing original data affect your imagination? Journal about your experiences and the stories that come to mind.

23

 ## *Bringing Your Memoir into the World*

> *And the day came when the risk it took to remain tight inside the bud was more painful than the risk it took to blossom.*
> —Anais Nin

Bringing your memoir into the world means traversing that invisible boundary line that protected you all along as you wrote your stories. Then you simply wrote, listened to your inner voice, and healed, as your first draft evolved. You completed the first stages of writing your memoir, described in Chapter 17: planting seeds, tending, designing. Now, after months or perhaps years of writing, the snippets and journal entries and vignettes and stories have become a larger story tied together with narrative structure and themes. Now you have the makings of a book.

Who Will Read Your Book?

First assess the risk. Imagine strangers and acquaintances and friends reading the intimate details you've written about your life. If you feel that your story is too personal to make public, or that you would feel too vulnerable, you may not want to share it or publish it. You do not have to do anything else with your accumulated writings, though you may want to go through at least the first draft just for your own satisfaction.

The rest of this chapter is addressed to those who do want to get their book out into the world. It takes you through the last two stages of creative writing: pruning and harvesting.

Re-Visioning

Re-visioning means rewriting. You will go through several drafts to get it where you want it to be. Begin by reading your first draft, considering it as a whole instead of a series of small pieces, making notes about how to proceed. A writing group or coach can help you go through this process of discovery and rediscovery. Listen to the book as it tells you what it needs to become whole.

Genre

For the purpose of healing, you have written the first draft as a memoir. Now it's time to decide whether your final version will be straight memoir or some combination of memoir, fiction, and/or poetry. Many novels are actually thinly disguised autobiography: *The Prince of Tides* by Pat Conroy, *The Joy Luck Club* by Amy Tan, *The House of the Spirits* by Isabel Allende, *Rumors of Peace* by Ella Leffland, *To the Lighthouse* by Virginia Woolf, and *Bastard Out of Carolina* by Dorothy Allison.

You may choose to fictionalize your memoir to protect your family, your friends, or yourself for ethical or legal reasons. As I said in Chapter 14, you must be certain that you do not defame anyone's character or invade the privacy of others in order to avoid libel. To prevent problems, consult an attorney who specializes in publishing law. An attorney can vet your manuscript (read it and note potential legal problems) and suggest ways to avert trouble.

If you decide to write a fictionalized version of your memoir, to avoid confusion in your own mind don't change characters' names until the final draft. Also, you must understand that memoir and fiction are critiqued and presented differently. For instance, the literal truth does not matter when considering plot, characters, and actions for fiction. However, truth is indeed stranger than fiction and the unbelievable aspects of real life must be changed when presented as fiction. The genre does not fare well with coincidence, bizarrely convenient events, or characters whose motivations are hard to understand. In memoirs, however, as in real life, such things happen all the time and can be justified by the statement, "This is hard to believe, but it is in fact true, and I stand behind its veracity."

If you decide to stay with pure memoir, then you should show your second or third draft to the people named in it and obtain their written consent before putting it in print. If you receive negative feedback, take it seriously. You may find it necessary to disguise someone's identity or even remove that character from the story. Again, consult an attorney to be safe.

Reworking the Drafts

• Consider your narrator's voice. Does he or she sound angry, grudging, or resentful? If the voice resonates with unresolved emotion, readers will find it more difficult to enter the story and stay with it. To solve this problem, write the raw story several times. The more you write it, the easier it will be for you to stand back and present it objectively, from a perspective that embraces all the characters. This is healing, as well as good writing. Your goal is to present a protagonist or narrator who sounds resolved or positive or neutral.

• Consider the characters in your book. The narrator and at least some of the other characters must appear sympathetic enough for readers to identify with. Readers need to feel they can step into the narrator's shoes and empathize with his or her actions and motivations even if they don't agree with them.

• How does your story move through time? If you find holes, you may need to add scenes to fill them in or you may need to add a paragraph here and there to smooth out transitions between scenes. If the story still feels incomplete, consider beginning or ending it at a different time.

• Where you begin and end can also depend on the size of your manuscript. Most books contain between 20,000 and 80,000 words. For practical reasons related to publishing costs, you may decide to shorten or lengthen your manuscript. But the integrity of your story should take precedence over such purely practical matters.

• Consider the pace of your book. Does the rate of movement in each scene fit the mood? Remember that you can speed up the pace through rapid bursts of dialogue, action, and quick movement from one incident to another. To slow down, use more description and narration in which you tell rather than show what happened.

• Consider the theme that ties your book together. Your reflections and summaries should present a unified philosophy that readers can identify and understand.

As you complete later drafts, you may feel overwhelmed and worried about the project. Ask for support from your writing coach and/or group. This is not a time to quit! Keep rewriting, chapter by chapter. It may take you a few months, but it gets done, one chapter at a time. As one of my students, Denise Roessle, wrote:

> *Joining a writing group was one of the best things I've done during this process. Writing is such a solitary pursuit. After a while it's as if you're working in a vacuum. You don't know if what you've written is good or bad or makes any sense at all, or if anyone else is going to be the least bit interested in what you have to say. We all need feedback, especially from other writers, and most especially from those who are also working on personal stories. It's scary at first, reading to a group of strangers. But in the end, it's the only way to learn what you're doing well, what could be improved, and how to grow as a writer.*
>
> *Encouragement is just as important. So many times I've been sick to death of my own words, wondering why the hell I ever thought I could write. Reading aloud to other writers on a regular basis and hearing their appreciation for what I've done makes all the difference. Sharing our struggles and solutions is invaluable. I come away from every session with renewed momentum to keep going.*

Roessle learned how to listen to her book, how to hear its wisdom and needs. Most of all, she had perseverance.

Throughout the rewriting stage, keep your enthusiasm up by imagining the cover of your book and creating a list of possible titles. Later, you can think about what makes a title and cover a winner in terms of the marketplace. For now, just have fun with it and dream about it.

Editors

The most important aspect of bringing your book into the world is to present your prose, your ideas, and your story in the best possible way and this means hiring an editor. Before you look for an agent or write a proposal or approach a publisher, you should hire a professional editor to guide you through the process of smoothing your manuscript into a marketable product.

Engage the services of an experienced book editor who performs both developmental (or substantive) editing and copyediting. Look for someone with whom you feel comfortable—even though, in this computer age, you may never meet in person. You want to work with someone who understands how to maintain your voice despite any changes he or she may make and who provides a contract that stipulates the editing will be performed on a work-for-hire basis, with all rights retained by you. Remember that it is your editor's job to tell you about problems in the manuscript, to point out or correct errors, and to make suggestions for improvement so don't take this feedback personally. A good editor makes you feel good about the changes being made.

Learning about Publishing

Many books can help you learn about the publishing world. Here are a few to get you started. Many have been revised. Be sure to consult the most recent editions.

The Prepublishing Handbook: What you should know before you publish your first book. Patricia J. Bell, Cat'sPaw Press

The Self-Publishing Manual: How to Write, Print and Sell Your Own Book. Dan Poynter, Para Publishing

The Writer's Legal Companion. Brad Bunnin and Peter Beren, Perseus Press

1001 Ways to Market Your Books. John Kremer, Open Horizons

Literary Agents: What They Do, How They Do It, and How to Find and Work with the Right One for You. Michael Larsen, Wiley Books

How to Write a Book Proposal. Michael Larsen, Writer's Digest Books

Write the Perfect Book Proposal: 10 Proposals That Sold and Why. Jeff Herman and Deborah M. Adams, John Wiley & Sons

Formatting & Submitting Your Manuscript. Jack Neff, Glenda Neff, Don Prues, Writer's Digest Books

Other ways to become informed about the publishing business include taking courses, attending conferences, and joining organizations and e-mail discussion lists. Use your favorite search engine to find a list of lists, then join all those that relate to publishing. For the first few weeks, just read the messages you receive; after you have a sense of the differences among the lists, you can choose to drop one or continue them all, and you can begin asking questions. The e-mail and online publishing community is one of the friendliest and most helpful there is.

The two organizations for independent publishers, Publishers Marketing Association (PMA) and Small Publishers Association of North America (SPAN), both offer excellent newsletters and learning opportunities. In many areas around the country, affiliated groups meet monthly and provide education and support for new publishers.

Remember, however, that it's best not to focus on publishing matters until you have finished your book.

Publishing Options

The publishing world is highly competitive and certain genres have ups and downs, like the stock market. One year memoir may be in, another year it is not. Nonetheless, every month new memoirs hit the bookstore shelves.

Time, money, and business experience factor into the decision about how to publish. Many people turn to independent publishing partly because modern technology makes it possible. You can establish your own publishing company, produce your own book, and get it out into the world more easily, more quickly, and less expensively than ever before. And you need not depend on the whims of an acquisitions editor or get involved with the politics of a large corporation. Of course you pay for all this freedom by footing the bills and taking the risks yourself. On the other hand, you also reap all the profits.

Many people want to be published by a large commercial company or a small literary house because they want to receive an advance, and they think they can count on promotion by an established company. Of course the advance offered to first-time authors with no claim to fame is generally small; it can range from about $500 to $15,000. *Writer's Market,* a yearly publication of Writer's Digest Books, lists publishers of all sizes and provides information about whether they accept manuscripts from first-time or unagented writers, the amounts of advances and royalties offered, and the amount of time between acceptance and publication (which generally ranges from twelve to eighteen months).

Most first-time authors do not receive the royal-road-to-fame treatment. Furthermore, regardless of whether a large New York house publishes your book or you publish it independently, you will have to publicize and promote it yourself. Think about it. Why do you suppose famous authors appear at your local bookstore? Their publishers expect them to participate in selling their books. Book tours, signings, and television interviews can be grueling, but they are an integral part of marketing to bookstores and the general reading public.

One alternative to finding a commercial or literary publisher is to engage a subsidy publishing company that, for a fee, will publish your book and print as few or as many copies as you need. Not all book distributors and retail outlets look favorably on such books or accept them for sale because many subsidy publishers exercise no editorial quality control. As a result you may find it more difficult to sell your book.

If you choose to join the growing ranks of independent publishers, you can follow a less traditional route and produce an e-book, which will have a limited distribution and readership, or you can produce a regular book in hard cover or paperback. If you go the traditional route, you can ask a printing company that uses digital technology to print a small number of books (PQN or "print quantity needed"). This is also called "Print On Demand" publishing. You may want only 25 or 250 copies at first. Of course, each copy in a small print run will cost more per copy than if you have them printed on a regular printing press.

Each of the many publishing options has advantages and disadvantages. Once you complete your writing and take the time to learn about the publishing world, you will know which option is best for you.

Endings and Beginnings

You deserve a pat on the back and congratulations for many reasons. You have taken the brave journey through the dark forest and have arrived at a new place.

When you write a healing memoir, one that probes the depth and breadth of your identity and sense of self, you will find yourself at a place different from where you began—and, as T. S. Eliot wrote, you will know the place for the first time. Take pride in your perseverance and courage, your discipline and determination to heal and to learn to tell the stories that are important to you, stories that may have saved your life. The journey no doubt took you to places within yourself that you did not plan to visit, and it may have caused you to stumble along the way. But you kept going steadfastly through the darkness and into the light.

There is more to your story, and more stories to come. Celebrate giving yourself the permission to hear your own voice, and in that process to become whole.

What we call the beginning is often the end
And to make an end is to make a beginning.
The end is where we start from.

—T.S. Eliot, *Four Quartets*

Inspiring Stories by Student Writers

The stories that follow were written by my students in various workshops. The writers were interested in capturing the stories that had shaped their lives. They wrote from the heart, and it shows. I am pleased to offer a few of the many stories that I have been privileged to read and coach over the years. These stories show that everyone can write a story!

This story was written during a twenty-minute exercise in one of my all-day workshops. Remember that the author had said she was "not a real writer."

The Prayer Man

By Patsy Pinkney Phillips

Dedicated to Wayne Narvis Phillips, Sr.,

my loving husband

"Pray about it. Just pray about it." That is what Mother always said. I was a young woman of 22. I was finally very comfortable with myself. For once in my life I felt fast and fine. Of course, I was still cautious and very conservative. But in Atlanta in 1973, the Bible Belt of the USA, I was fast and fine. After all, I just graduated from UC Berkeley. Everyone in the world would expect me to be fast. Berkeley was known the world over for its drug culture, flower children, orgies, pot-smoking lectures, and hippies on every corner.

Of course all I had to do was say, "I'm from Berkeley," and folks would think of me as "fast, cool, on the cutting edge." So, in Atlanta I felt different, sophisticated, even a fashion statement. Well, I knew that I could keep them guessing. One day I would wear a miniskirt, knee-high suede boots, and Afro puffs. The next day a maxi, no bra, and a head rag. Dangling earrings, bright red and orange. What a fashion statement. I was sure no one would call me conservative or cautious. After all, I was miles away from family and friends. I was really on my own. Finding my own way.

It didn't take me long to realize that I was lonely. I was like a fish out of water, charting new territory. Finally sailing on my own, but too cautious to venture far from the shoreline.

I wanted a family like Mother's. I wanted a husband, a nice Christian man to marry. I could have a family and a career, but central to my desires was finding the "right man."

Mother was always there for me to talk to about this concern. But no matter where we started talking, she would always end up by saying, "Just pray about it." Then, as if I had never heard the story before, she would tell me again how she met Daddy. Mother would start off telling me how she was raised with her mother, sister, and a very mean stepfather. She shared how she longed to marry a good Christian man to take her away from all of that. She would pray and pray for this man. Then, every night she would dream and see this man, but she would never see his face. One day she prayed that the Lord would let her see his face. Mother would make a point to let me know that she only asked to see his face. For some reason, Mother wanted to make sure I understood that her desire for this man was holy and pure. Mother would emphasize each time she told the story that she saw him only above the waist.

After emphasizing the purity of her desire, she would continue to share how Aunt Earlene, a high school classmate, shared with her how she thought Mother and her brother would be perfect for each other. As the story goes, Aunt Earlene showed Mother a picture of my father, and to Mother's amazement the photo was a portrait of the man in her dreams. Mother wrote to this man. Mother and Daddy wrote to each other, dated, and got married.

So, according to Mother, I only had to pray and the Lord would send me the right man for me to marry. "Pray about it, just pray about it!" she would say. I would always respectfully assure Mother that I would pray about it, and then I would hang up the phone.

I would hopelessly, quietly review my inventory of past dates and future prospects of available single men. My list wasn't that long. After five minutes, I would call my girlfriends and we would go out on the town.

Back at work, as secretary for the university's African-American department, I was the first person to receive student requests for registration information. I spent a lot of time arranging the registration of new students.

Now, finally, on the first day of classes, I was able to put faces to the names of the students who had written for information all year long. I purposely wore my lime green head rag, halter top, green and orange platform shoes, and maxi with orange ear-boobs. I expected to be noticed. I don't remember much about that day except for this one student who came in.

It seemed that every student wore horn-rimmed glasses, a white pressed shirt, a black tie, and a suit jacket. In my five-inch platforms, I towered over all of the students. Since I was their first stop in the registration process, I quickly sent them on their way.

There was only one student who stood out above the rest. He was taller than me, wore a dashiki and a large Afro, and had a huge mustache. I remembered this student. I looked up and gave him a very long smile. I said, "May I help you?" Of course I could help him: I was the first stop. I gave him his papers and told him to go next door to see Dr. Long. I also told him to come right back after talking to Dr. Long. I was waiting for him. I waited and waited, and he did not come back. I sure hoped I'd see him again.

Mother would say, "You only have to mumble to say a little prayer." Well, I guess that was one little prayer, because that afternoon when I had to deliver the mail and stop by financial aid, guess who I saw? Yes, as I stood in the financial aid line this tall, fine man from registration walked toward me. He had a very serious look on his face. I thought, He doesn't scare me. So boldly I said, "How're you doing?" He looked around, as if not knowing who I was talking to. I kept staring at him with a smile. He stopped, smiled, and said, "Do I know you?"

I smiled back at him. "You don't remember me. I guess you thought I just worked here. I am the secretary from registration this morning."

I told him I was also a student working on my master's degree. And then he asked me where I was from.

"I'm from Berkeley." From the smile on his face I could tell exactly what he was thinking. Oh yes, he thought I was fast and fine.

The next thing I knew, Wayne Phillips came by my office regularly. We dated and spent hours just talking. We had similar backgrounds, with similar values and family rules. I felt as if I had known him all my life.

What made things perfect for me was the next Thanksgiving. I didn't have enough money to go home, so I was just planning on having a very lonely holiday all by myself. Wayne wasn't planning on going home for Thanksgiving either, so we decided to celebrate together. We shopped for our food together and prepared our meal together. So far away from home, I felt at home with this man. I didn't have to spend Thanksgiving alone.

Four months later Wayne asked me to marry him. We got married in the little chapel on campus. Two years ago, after twenty-five years of marriage, three children, and two grandchildren, we renewed our vows. This was the man of my prayers.

❋

Nutmeg
By Nancy Grimley Carleton

I didn't want Nutmeg to be my rabbit, but she insisted.

I was taking care of her for a friend who was having some construction done on her house and didn't want her new rabbit terrified by the noise.

I gave Nutmeg food and water every day and was amused by the way she claimed her territory in the room where she was staying. But all my focus was on my beloved Willow, a gray Netherland dwarf rabbit like Nutmeg, whom I had been nursing through an illness.

Nutmeg lived with us during the last month of Willow's life, and when Willow died during surgery, Nutmeg set out on a mission to claim the rabbit position in my household.

I wasn't interested.

I was grieving the loss of Willow, who had had such a special quality about him that even his battle-hardened veterinarian wept when he died.

I thought it would be a long time before I'd be ready to get another rabbit. But Nutmeg had other ideas and set about winning me over with more determination than the most ardent lover. She ignored my partner, Susan, and focused on me, since I was clearly the rabbit person in the house. Day by day, this small three-pound rabbit pursued me, hopping over full of bunny kisses whenever I entered the room.

I resisted for almost a month, but then, when the construction at my friend's home was finally complete, I started to realize that I didn't really want Nutmeg to go. And when Diane arrived to pick her up, Nutmeg absolutely refused to get in the carrier. She ran away from Diane and jumped onto my lap. "Well, it looks like she plans to stay here," Diane said, gracefully accepting reality. And from that point on, Nutmeg was my rabbit and I was her person.

Nutmeg continued to show that she knew what she wanted and exactly how to get it. Her next mission was to become a mother. She needed a mate to achieve her goal, and she was determined to let me know.

By now she was living in my bedroom and, since there was no other rabbit around, Nutmeg began to court me, rabbit style. At night, when I crawled under the comforter, Nutmeg would jump up on the bed and hop back and forth over my head for hours on end while making a humming sound. After several sleepless nights, I set up a barrier of cushions to keep her away, but she managed to push them aside and continue her nightly hopping. The humming was hypnotic; it felt as if she were casting a spell over me.

I can't really say whether it was the spell or just that I was getting more and more exhausted, but after a week of this sleep deprivation I found myself purchasing a black male Netherland dwarf bunny with white highlights. Although he was only seven weeks old, Nutmeg began making her desires aggressively known the moment Blackberry appeared. The hopping back and forth over the head while humming was indeed a rabbit courtship ritual, and I watched as Nutmeg now directed it toward Blackberry. I had to appreciate her discernment, however, for she had spared me what I learned was the final component of the ritual: urine spraying.

Although at seven weeks Blackberry wasn't quite mature enough to father a litter, in five more weeks he was, and Nutmeg was soon pregnant. She pulled out her soft gray fur to make a nest in preparation, and a month later gave birth to four babies.

Once the babies were born, Nutmeg showed me that the person who coined the phrase "fierce as a mother lion" must not have known about rabbits. I'd never known that rabbits could growl, but Nutmeg would growl and lunge at the legs of any stranger who got too close to her litter. If she knew she weighed only three pounds, she wasn't letting on.

Nutmeg made it clear that once I'd named the four babies—Parsley, Juniper, Hazel, and Shasta—I could never give them away, and she presided as matriarch over my rabbit family of six for the next eight years.

Toward the end of 1998, when Nutmeg was eight years old, I noticed that her eyes had started to bulge and her breathing was getting harder. X-rays revealed that she had an inoperable tumor near her heart, the result of a genetic anomaly that I would eventually learn all her children shared. Prednisone could slow the process, but no cure was possible.

Nutmeg would never be one to suffer and decline slowly to a state of incapacity. She was too strong-willed and far too dignified for that.

I talked to Nutmeg every day and let her know that while I wanted her to stay with me as long as she could, I didn't want her to suffer, and I knew she'd know when to leave. But I had one request: I wanted to be with her when she died.

In the wild, rabbits usually go off by themselves to die, or let down their guard so a predator can take care of it for them. And house rabbits often go off by themselves too, dying when there's no one around. Because I hadn't been able to be with Willow when he died, it felt especially important to me to be with Nutmeg. Intuitively I knew that she did not need any assistance dying, and that a trip to the vet for euthanasia would not be necessary.

One afternoon in January, I came into my bedroom, where Nutmeg and Blackberry still lived. The midwinter sun shone weakly through the window. Nutmeg was lying on her side in an uncharacteristic position, but otherwise seemed fine, and hopped over to greet me as usual.

I sensed her telling me that she was ready to go, and that all I needed to do was hold her.

I got into bed with Nutmeg in my arms, and she lay on my chest as the winter light faded. Her heart beat strongly against my own, and her warm, alfalfa-scented bunny breath caressed my cheek. I stroked her soft gray fur, and she kissed my chin. As the minutes passed, I felt her body slowly softening as her legs started to go limp and then stiffen. Her breathing began to come in quick gasps, but she kept kissing my face, her tongue like a whispering feather. As the tears streamed down, I told her what a wonderful bunny she had been, what a good mommy to her babies. For two hours, I told her how grateful I was for all she'd given me, and I felt her love and gratitude flowing back.

Then the image came to me of her spirit leaping out of her body, and at that very moment, her body leapt in my arms, from my chest to my shoulder, and she died.

Although I was crying, I experienced an incredible sense of joy at the same time. I breathed deeply, and the air entered my lungs like an embrace. Nutmeg sent me an image of herself leaping in a beautiful meadow filled with the fresh green grass of springtime.

By allowing me to be with her and by dying naturally in my arms, Nutmeg taught me that death is nothing to fear. It is just a leap from here to there, a simple movement toward the realm of spirit. This was a greater gift than I could ever have imagined, and it served me in good stead when I faced a diagnosis of a rare and potentially life-threatening disease of my own later that same year.

Never again would I see a need to take a rabbit to be euthanized. They know perfectly well how and when to let go. And between that January, when Nutmeg died, and the end of the year when I received my diagnosis, three more of my rabbits would die naturally in my arms—Parsley, Juniper, and finally Nutmeg's mate, Blackberry—all cheered on by Nutmeg, fearlessly showing them the way home.

❋

Johanna wrote this during an all-day workshop. In this vignette written in thirty minutes, she paints a picture of grief, of silence. She presents such a vivid world of color and sensual detail that we feel we are standing behind her, watching, feeling the family's grief and loneliness that will haunt this young girl for years.

Bim
By Johanna Clark

It was in 1942 that my mother received the telegram. These were the war years. My father and two of my brothers were in the navy. Life on the home front seemed to revolve around the war effort, food rationing, and victory gardens, and around news from the Atlantic or Pacific fronts.

I had just turned four. My father had by now, as they said, "lost all the money." The family had moved to a smaller house on what was called the wrong side of town. My mother's and father's marriage, the second for my mother, was strained. Her central attachment was to her first-born, the boy called Bim. Bim was her golden child. He was a handsome blond fighter pilot who had been her hope and protector during her earlier years of single motherhood.

When the telegram was delivered to our door, my mother clutched it and sank to her knees. This might otherwise have been an ordinary morning. Sunlight streamed through the living room window and dappled the faded oriental carpet. My mother was in a housedress, her light blond hair swept up in the style of the '40s. She was a small woman, with a plumpness she would lose later, when she became sick. I stood on the side of the room, a scraggly little blond girl, hair in pigtails, wearing overalls that were too small for me.

I moved toward her instant grief. She tightened and was at that moment pulled further into a world apart from me. The morning light was the same, and the rug still bathed in its radiance, and she was moving away.

The telegram said that Bim, Rufus Campion Clark, was

reported missing in action. His plane probably went down somewhere in the South Pacific. His body was never recovered.

After the day of the telegram, my mother hung a special
memorial cloth in the front window, as was the custom, the gold
star indicating that a young man was not to return.

In time, my father and my brother Neal did return. My
sister, Lee, married her boyfriend who was back from the army.
And we moved again, my parents, my brother Smitty and I,
back to a rented house on the West Side.

My mother commissioned a neighbor to paint a large portrait of Bim from photographs. The portrait showed a smiling
and handsome Bim in naval uniform, against a blue sky. It was
put in a gold frame and hung over the fireplace mantle. Brass
candlesticks were placed on either side. And my mother had all
the downstairs rooms painted blue, to go with the blues of the
portrait. Upstairs, all the wallpapers were in blues.

By 1945 the war was over and my parents' marriage went
through a final couple of years of breakdown before it dissolved,
before my father disappeared in defeat and my mother went back
to work to support Smitty and me, her late-in-life children.

We didn't talk much about Bim at the dinner table, Mother,
Smitty, and I. In fact, I don't recall Mother ever mentioning
him. I do remember the bottom drawer of her oak desk, stuffed
with carefully wrapped letters, her correspondence with Bim
throughout his college and war years. My mother's letters were
neatly typed on her old Royal. Respecting her privacy, I never
read the letters.

My mother stayed behind her veil of sadness and sorrow.
Sometimes she would sit and read or listen to music on Sunday
afternoons in the living room near the painting. But mostly
she was occupied with her six-day-a-week job at the store,
and Smitty and I constructed our own lives, separate from our
mother and separate from each other as well.

After a few years, when I was eleven and Smitty fourteen,
our mother became sick and had the first of several surgeries for
cancer. She lived for another three years.

When she died, there was still the painting of Bim. My

sister had returned from her home in California to clear out the house. She destroyed Bim's and my mother's correspondence, but she took the painting back to California and hung it over her own mantle and painted her walls blue. She lives in another state now, and Bim's portrait is still over her mantle.

A few years ago her younger brother, Neal, told Lee that he'd resolved so many of his conflicted feelings toward Bim and wanted to borrow the painting. Lee said that she couldn't part with it, that she spoke with Bim every day. She sent Neal a Xerox® copy.

I often think about the Bim shrine that my mother erected and that my sister perpetuated. And I think of how the Bim painting froze a real young man into eternal glory, a prince forever. But mostly I think of that ordinary, brilliant morning when my mother sank to her knees into a life of grief and disconnection and of how, even as a four year old, I knew that it was one of those moments that would change the lives of everyone in the family.

❋

Laura's story transported the class into a world we had never seen, heard, or tasted before, into another country and culture, weaving for us a magic world of dreams and wishes, which sometimes come true.

The Wish
By Laura Sheehan

In 1979, I was working in India for the international clothing company Esprit. I had gone to Delhi to start over, yet again. I was fleeing a mess that I had gotten myself into at my previous job in Korea. Things in Seoul had gotten very complicated. I was working long hours to build the leather jacket import business owned by my boyfriend. He spent part of his time in Seoul with me and part of his time in LA. Suddenly, the company went bankrupt. At the time they shut down, I was left with thousands of dollars in unpaid salary and a gigantic hotel bill. I ended up having to pay it myself just to get out of there. Oh, and the boyfriend had run off with his new secretary in the LA office, forgetting to mention to me that he no longer owned the company. He had sold his shares to the other investors for a dollar, and disappeared without a word.

So my track record with men was not good. He wasn't the first guy to let me down, either. I had always been more the friend type than the girlfriend type. I didn't always have a man around. In fact, I had already spent years alone. The fact that my parents were divorced only increased my fatalistic view of romance and marriage. I figured I wasn't lucky in love. I was thirty-one years old and absolutely certain that I would never get married.

After the disastrous ending of my time in Korea, I felt like a complete idiot for having been taken for such a ride. I made a decision. This time I was not going waste any time beating myself up. Getting into scrapes was a part of life.

Now, I figured I had two choices: I could get depressed or I could get busy. I decided to just call this the bottom and start planning my move up. Things could hardly get any worse. And above all, I wouldn't tell *anyone* what had happened – not my parents, not my friends. If I didn't tell anybody, no one would know about it, and maybe it would seem as if it had never really happened.

I called my friend who was working at Esprit in Hong Kong, wangled an interview with Doug Tompkins, the owner, and hopped on a plane. The meeting went very well. I was offered a job on the spot after telling Doug about all my fabulously successful work experience in Korea, leaving out a few pesky details. Three months later, Doug transferred me to India.

So now, six months after what I can only describe as the nadir of my existence, I was living in India, in the Esprit company house in Delhi with five servants, a cook, two maids, two gardeners, and a chauffer-driven car, thoroughly enjoying the colonial lifestyle.

The thing is, it is actually quite easy to go around in life getting yourself into total messes. And after those bad experiences, which you know you have somehow created, you start carrying this tragic idea of yourself around in your head, which of course seems completely logical. So you go on projecting this idea of yourself into the future. But in reality, this picture of the future is only an image. So even though I had bounced back pretty well, I still had the idea that I would never get married floating around in my head. The secret is, we are what we think, so to change your future, you just have to change your thinking.

But sometimes you also need a little extra help from the cosmos. Sometimes, you can find yourself in a special moment that breaks a pattern that you have lived with your whole life, a pattern you are convinced is your destiny or at the very least an ingrained personality trait. At this moment, at this intersection of space and time, you suddenly notice that something is different. If you are paying attention and are truly awake, something magical can happen.

This special moment happened to me sometime in March 1979, soon after I came to India. On a day off, one of the Indian girls in the office offered to take me sightseeing. We took a boat over to a small island in the Bay of Bombay, to a famous cave called Elephanta. She said it was known for its ancient stone carvings.

The sky was overcast with a kind of golden yellow haze so typical of India. We boarded a funky old ferry boat jam-packed with Indian families and went chugging off over the choppy, grey water, the boat rocking back and forth with the weight of so many people. Besides my friend and I, the boat was filled with women in bright saris with children clutching onto their skirts, and men in dark business suits.

Teenage boys in long white tunics, called kurta pajamas, holding hands or hanging their arms over each others shoulders, leaning against each other, like boys do all over Asia. Groups of beautiful twenty-something girls with chiseled features, and large brown eyes framed in unbelievably long eyelashes with jet-black braids down their backs, leaned against the side of the boat. They clustered together giggling, in their colorful traditional clothes, bursting with fuschias, pinks, emerald greens, their white teeth flashing against their warm brown skin. Everyone was pressed against everyone else and not caring. This ride cost ten cents and took a half an hour.

We reached the island and piled off the boats onto the gangplank, pushed along by the flow of bodies onto a wide dirt path, moving slowly up the hill. At the opening of the caves, we walked up the small stone stairs at the entrance and stepped inside. The light spilled from outside onto the ground part of the way into the mouth of the cave, illuminating only the entrance. After being so long in the bright sun on the boat, at first it was so dark that we couldn't see anything. We had to stand still a minute for our eyes to adjust to the darkness. Gradually, carved figures materialized on the cave walls. The cave was supported by massive circular stone columns more than two feet in diameter carved right out of the rock ceiling. They followed one after another across the cavern.

"This cave was carved in the eighth century," my friend said solemnly.

The work was breathtaking. I walked through the caverns admiring the sensual curvilinear bodies. The sheer number of carvings was stunning. One after another, there were scenes of gods and goddesses, bodies intricately intertwined. They stood relaxed and practically nude under twisted leafy vines studded with lotuses. Peeking out from under the vines were graceful stone animals – rats, miniature elephants, and monkeys. I tried to imagine the sculptors in the eighth century working half in the dark, chiseling out such perfect bodies and faces, painstakingly carving these voluptuous bodies out of solid rock, rock they made look just like flesh. These were passionate and sensual gods.

On each sculpture were places that were black and smooth from eight centuries of people stroking them with their fingers in passing, hoping to feel their power. I turned the corner at the edge of a colonnade. As I walked down the rows to the end I could see an enormous triptych set back into an alcove. It was a magnificent three-headed bust rising twenty feet tall and spanning twenty feet wide. The main head faced forward, and growing out of each side was another head facing sideways. The central figure was wearing an ornately carved helmet-like headdress taller than his face, stylistically shaped like a seashell coiling back over his head. He was covered in what might have been gold jewelry. His earlobes stretched down, weighted with earrings attached to a three-strand beaded necklace lying across his bare chest. All of this was carved out of the same block of stone. His lips were full. His eyes were wide open with a look of Buddha-like calm. The head on the right side had a soft expression, with long carved stone curls peeking out from under the headdress, and appeared to be a woman. The head on the left side was more severe looking and appeared to be a man.

The way the cave arched over his head gave the viewer a chance to have his own private moment with the figure, which was set on a stone platform. At the bottom was a stone semi-circle filled with water. At the bottom of the pool I could see coins glistening. Coins from all over the world.

"That's Shiva. See the three faces. The face looking at you is the Creator, the face of Eternity. Look – on this side, you will see the Preserver and on the other side, the Destroyer." My friend stood behind me, speaking reverently in a low voice.

"Make a wish. It will be granted," she whispered in my ear.

"This is a holy place." She walked away discreetly to leave me alone with Shiva.

I looked down at all the coins in the water and thought about all the people who had passed through here asking for their secret desires. If this was a special place, a holy place where wishes could be granted, what should I wish for?

I looked into Shiva's large, clear, wide-open eyes. He looked right back at me, powerful and mysterious.

I paused, my eyes still locked with his. *I must be careful to do this right*, I thought. *If I make a wish, and I want it to be granted, I must make it in the right way. I must be sure to wish for the right thing.*

I thought for a moment. *It can't be a selfish wish. Or a greedy wish. I'm sure it has to be a pure wish to be granted.*

I asked myself, *what do I want most in life?*

I took a coin out of my purse.

I waited and closed my eyes, cupping my hands together, closing my palms over my coin. I bowed my head and raised my hands to the figure and slowly phrased my wish in my mind.

I wish…I may no longer be alone. I wish…for a companion in life. I wish…for someone I can give myself to, to share with.

Looking into the eyes of Shiva, I opened my eyes, uncupped my hands, and threw my coin into the water. It drifted to the bottom of the pool and glistened back at me, nestled among all the other wishes.

In the moment before I made the wish, I realized that for my wish to be granted, I could not just wish to get married, or for a perfect man. I could not present a list of conditions that would have to be met. I could not specify what this companion should look like or be like. I was only asking to *not be alone*, and if I was willing to give whatever I had to give, then maybe it wouldn't be so hard for the Creator, Preserver, Destroyer to grant my wish. And maybe since my heart was pure, when my wish was granted I would be able to recognize it, because I wouldn't be looking for the wrong things, projecting an image from my past. I would just be open and pure and ready for something good to happen.

A week later my wish was granted. I met my future husband.

He is Indian.

We have been happily married for twenty-six years.

Small sketches can say so much about how life is lived and the meaning we give it. The following vignettes, set in Iran, are small jewels. Strung together, they weave a tapestry of images and memories from a different place and time. Roya Sakhai, a psychotherapist in Berkeley, California, teaches at New College.

Madarjun and Her Opium
By Roya Sakhai

My madarjun, my grandmother, was a very strong woman. She was a large woman with beautiful black hair and tiny red-black lips, thick black eyebrows, and big brown eyes.

My most vivid memory of her is the daily opium smoking. The ritual of putting all kinds of nuts and pastries and teas on different dishes, and of course the little tea pot with small tea glasses. She smoked opium four or five times a day. It seems like those four or five times of smoking, her sweet ritual, was all she had to live for. I can not exactly remember what she wore. I have this image of pale yellow flannel cotton, something between a nightgown and a housedress.

Morning would start with her slow move to the downstairs room to set up all she needed to start the ritual. She would put chucks on a *manghal*, a special tray for the opium, fire the chucks, and start the opium. She'd have a puff of opium and a sip of tea, then eat some biscuits to cut the bitter opium taste.

She would start in a very bad mood, then switch to a better mood through the day as the opium started to work on her body and mind. When she started to get high, she would call us, my brother and me, to come to the room and sit by her manghal to listen to her stories . . .

❊

Madarjun's Co-Wives
By Roya Sakhai

You could see the passage of time in Madarjun's life from being a co-wife to divorcing two times and being a modern woman.

One of Madarjun's most interesting stories was about her first marriage. She married three times, but none of the marriages were as interesting as the first one. She always kept the elegant frame with Grandpa's photo in the cupboard in her room. Once in a while she would bring the photo out. She would kiss it, and cry some, and then put the frame back in the cupboard. Every time the photo came out, I would hear a new piece of her life.

She was twelve years old when she became the youngest wife of my grandpa. He was from Afghanistan, a diplomat. He'd travel to Iran, India, and Pakistan, and would marry a new wife each time he went on a new trip. Grandma said she was his last wife, and, according to her, he adored her.

Madarjun told me that Grandpa, arriving in Ahwaz, a city in the south of Iran, had asked for the most beautiful girl in the town, and everyone recommended Madarjun. This was how she became his last wife. He sent for her hand with lots of jewelry and silk, and her father agreed to the marriage.

Grandpa had many, many other wives whom he had married during his other trips. The fun part of this story was that Grandma was still best friends with many of these co-wives decades after Grandpa's death. My brother and I would call them "aunts" and listen to their memories.

Grandma would tell us how much fun she had with her co-wives. How much they loved each other. She said, "Grandpa would bring lots of silk from India, and we would share the silk." She had a sweet laugh, and a shine would come to her eyes as she said, "Of course being the youngest and the most favorite wife, I would get most of the silk, but I was not selfish. I would share the silk with all of your aunts."

In this story of heartrending family separation, the author sets the scene and uses the senses to show how the children experienced this traumatic moment that changed the lives of everyone in the family forever.

The Departure
By Geraldine Messina Smith

My sisters and I watched from the front window of our house on Josephine Street as a black car pulled up in front and stopped. A woman wearing a dark coat and carrying a black handbag and black notebook got out and walked to our door.

I hoped this wasn't the social worker Daddy said would come for us. She had gray hair, wore glasses but no lipstick, and had on old-fashioned shoes with thick heels. Her thin lips made her look stern. Maybe she was expecting to have a fight with Daddy. I knew he did not want us taken away from him. Daddy bent his head down as he came to the door. The lady stood with her coat on and refused his invitation to sit down. She said, "Are the girls ready? They do not need to take anything with them. They will be getting clothes and shoes at the orphanage."

I was twelve years old, and I had heard about this orphanage. I thought only children with no parents were orphans, and I could not understand how we could be taken to an orphanage when we had parents, but I was afraid to ask questions. My little sisters clustered around me, and I tried to be strong for them.

The lady ushered the four of us down the stairs. Daddy hung his head and followed us. Why didn't he say anything? He was still in his dirty work clothes, with cement still sticking to his khaki-colored shirt and pants. I looked up at him—he had always seemed so tall and strong, I knew he was proud of his strength. He had to be strong for his work at Mondo Construction Company, paving streets, sidewalks, and driveways, digging ditches for sewer pipes, and laying bricks for foundations. I was surprised to see tears streaming down his ruddy, weather-beaten face. This was the first time we had seen him cry. He was still a handsome man with his black curly hair and rugged face, but today his shoulders were hunched. Today he did not seem strong. He was sad, broken down, and upset. Our family was being broken up just because Momma had been taken to the state mental hospital, and he could not prevent it.

Charlotte was just three, and Doris was five. They began crying, too. I was stoic and kept myself from crying by clenching my teeth and tightening my lips. I needed to take care of my sisters as I was used to doing. Rosalie, aged ten, had a very frightened look on her face, but she did not cry until Daddy hugged and kissed her as he in turn hugged each of us. He stroked Rosalie's curly auburn hair, and then she began to cry.

He leaned down to hug and kiss Doris and gently tug her pigtails. She began sobbing, "Daddy, I want to stay home with you." Charlotte picked up the refrain and cried louder, "Me too, Daddy." He picked up Charlotte and hugged her, stroking her light brown, kinky hair.

He said, "You gotta go with Jerry, Rosalie, and Doris to the orphanage. I'll come see you. You are my *'piccialidda*,'" my little girl.

Doris clung to one leg and Charlotte hung on the other, but Daddy released their grips, took their hands, and walked the four of us to the social worker's car. Charlotte was carrying the doll Mom had made for her out of some rags. There had never been enough money to buy dolls or other toys, so this doll was special.

The social worker said, "Okay girls, climb in. It's time to go."

One by one we crawled into the back seat. Charlotte and Doris were still crying as I helped them step up into the car. All four of us huddled together in the back seat, clinging to each other. Rosalie was drying her tears on her dress, trying to act very grown up by not crying. My eyes were watering, but I fought back my tears. We worried about Daddy being left all alone. He came and stood next to the car, took his red handkerchief from his back pocket, and dried his tears.

He leaned over and said, "*Stata tenda*." Take care. He was always telling us to do that. The social worker slammed the door, and we all jumped. Before she got into the driver's seat, he asked, "You sure I visit my children? Promesa, they come home some Sundays?" When he was upset and tried to speak in English, he would mix up his English and Italian.

She reassured him in a voice that sounded annoyed. "Yes, Mr. Messina, you can visit some evenings and every weekend, and you can even take them home sometimes." He shook his head as if he was unsure of whether he could trust her words.

As we drove away, I realized that none of the neighbors had come to say good-bye, though they were probably watching us from behind the curtains in their front rooms. I wondered if we would ever see them again or if we'd be able to come home.

❋

Audrey's memoir began as a poem, fragments of memory and story, eventually woven together to form a whole, healing piece. There are many beginnings, and each person has his or her own process in getting a work to its full form.

The Grandmothers
(Excerpt from: *Nothing Left Standing but the Frame*)
by Audrey Martin

At the age of twenty-five, I called Evanston Hospital and asked them to release my medical records. Ten years had passed since my incarceration on their locked psychiatric ward. I began writing *Nothing Left Standing but the Frame,* drawing on poems, journals, and records of those years. My first draft of my memoir read like a long, anorexic poem. Written in poetic prose, it was thin and narrow on the page. Wanting to give voice to the turmoil of my adolescence, I completed the memoir this year. As an experienced psychotherapist, I am clear that writing my story has not only brought closure for me, but can help others struggling with anorexia and those treating them, to gain a deeper understanding of this life-threatening disease.

I was a very small girl to begin with, and I experienced my size early on as a focal point of other people's attention. There was something about being petite and delicate that was of value to them, and therefore to me. The women in my family were buxom and curvaceous, except for my grandmother, Sophie, who was thin and angular and forever fretting about her size, which she believed to be gargantuan, even though she weighed ninety-three pounds. She restricted her intake of food, punctuating conversations at mealtime with "*Oy vay iz mir,*" and walking miles each day after eating to burn off calories.

We lived in a two-flat on Custer Street in Evanston. My father's parents, Sophie and Max, owned our building and lived downstairs with my aunt and my cousin Deborah, ten months younger than I. Grandma Sophie's energy was boundless.

Always in motion, she moved at hummingbird pace, cleaning, arranging furniture, putting everything in proper order. She was a horrible cook—with a dreaded chicken paprikash her one staple meal at family gatherings. Mostly, my grandmother subsisted on Manichewitz whole wheat matzo, dry, one cracker sheet broken in two on her plate, green salad with dietetic dressing, and black coffee, Maxwell House, by the potful.

In contrast, my maternal grandmother, Ida, ambulated with slow deliberation. An excellent cook and baker, she represented the redolence of old world and new in her kitchen, with sweet and complex smells emanating from her always busy stove. Her body, soft, round, bones muted by tender flesh, was my refuge. At her table there was whole milk in glass jars with cream at the top, and sweet cream butter floating in pools over hot farina at breakfast. In almost every room, of which there were many, little glass or porcelain dishes filled with candies and nuts were there for the taking. A stop in the dining room for a nonpareil, a handful of pistachios, red die stains forming in a child's sweaty palms; there were no secrets for there was nothing to hide.

Most Sundays we gathered at my mother's parents' home with aunts and uncles and cousins to partake in rich Jewish feasts, taking pleasure in the cornucopia of delight my grandmother had created.

It wasn't long before I began receiving attention for the amount of food I consumed. "You eat like a little *fegela*," I'd hear my aunt chuckle from the table. "What are you having tonight, a chicken wing and a lettuce leaf?" Everyone would laugh. My reputation as a small eater was an anomaly in my mother's family, where voracious appetites were the norm and competition for food was a playful part of family meals. I would shrug my shoulders and smile as platters of roasted chicken, beef brisket and farfel were consumed, followed by carrots glazed with brown sugar, steaming rolls of kishke and iceberg lettuce salads with cherry tomatoes, cucumber slices resting on plates.

My mother's kitchen was vacuous by comparison to my

Grandma Ida's, and abundant in relation to Grandma Sophie's. In our home, my father's whims ruled our palettes. Absorbed by a passion for fitness, there was an absence of sugar and an emphasis on health food, which other members of my extended family found amusing. Jokes about having to hunt for anything fun to eat would often be told when they came to visit. There was a feeling that we were different; it was seductive to live on less. I became very interested in nutrition and in fasting, which easily segued into not eating at all for extended periods of time. Going hungry meant teetering on the edge. Tempted by deprivation, hunger brought me closer to something I did not fully understand.

I was a member of a family in which the role of survival was implicit; holocaust stories are a part of my earliest remembrances. Although only my paternal grandmother Sophie lost family during the war, both of my parents' families were of Russian ancestry and stories of the *pogroms* that ran through villages where they lived were related in hushed tones after dinner, sitting with the adults over dessert and coffee.

"We are the chosen ones," Aunt Berta would whisper under her breath. I knew that something horrible had befallen her as a young girl, soldiers pillaging the homes and shops on her street, committing unthinkable crimes.

"She died of melancholia." Grandma Ida shook her head back and forth while she spoke, as if to attempt to erase the memory of Devorah, the aunt I knew only from this one story, of her sitting upright in the dark, in my grandmother's bed, shredding the bed sheets while she cried.

"Blood is thicker than water," Grandma Sophie said to the table, while looking squarely at me. This I understood to mean that above all else, family loyalty was the key to our survival. And in between the lines: "You should marry a nice Jewish boy."

There were other stories that were not meant for me to hear. I'd turn my ear to the adult conversation, only to be met with: "The *kinder*, the *kinder*," meaning, not for a child's ears. I would feign disinterest, wandering just far enough away that they'd begin their stories again. And I listened.

"He ate crackers for dinner, that's all he had for months after he left Russia."

"We lived on nothing, *nothing* to our names."

"We have plenty now, *kineahora*," warding off the evil eye.

They believed it could strike again at any time. I hid my fascination with hunger from them. Yet I knew that going without was something they could understand.

❋

This was one of Francie's early stories, written shortly after her mother died. She told me that it came from remembering a tiny detail, the pattern of the linoleum floor. Out of this small detail, a whole memory flooded forward that had been repressed. Once she was able to form the memory into words, she was standing in a new place in herself.

Cowboys, Indians, and the Fort
By Francie L.

The four silver metallic legs of the light grey formica-topped table defined the "safe" area of our fort. The table top over our heads enclosed and protected from above. The black linoleum tiles with the small flecks of color on the floor were cool to the touch, smooth and slippery. My sister, brother and I wanted to drag one of the blankets off the bed to drape over the table so we could have walls to our fort, but mom wouldn't let us. Everything outside of the area defined by the table was Indian territory and dangerous.

As cowboys, we would venture out from the fort to explore. When the Indians attacked, we retreated to the safety of the fort, just like they did on TV.

Our game of Cowboys and Indians was interrupted by mom calling us to drink soup made of dried *bok choy* (Chinese chard) that she said was good for us. It smelled bad. My older brother, five years old, refused to drink it. Laughing as if it were a joke and emboldened by his example, my sister and I refused also.

Mom tried to coax us to drink it. If we drank it real fast, it wouldn't taste bad, she told us. It was good for us. She made it especially for us.

When we could not be coaxed into it, and refused again, Mom got the wooden yardstick. The one she hit us with. Unlike the wimpy yardsticks of today that snap in two under a little pressure, the yardstick of 1953 was thick, sturdy and unbreakable. Wisely, Rick and Beth drank their soup after a couple of whacks on the legs.

The whacks hurt and my legs smarted, but I still refused to drink the foul-smelling soup. Mom held Rick and Beth up as examples of good, obedient children because they drank the soup. Stubbornly, I refused again. She whacked me a couple more times. Scared and trying to be brave at the same time, I ran under the table to the safety of our fort. She ignored the imaginary walls of the fort and dragged me out by my leg. The smooth floor gave my small hands nothing to grab onto and did nothing to slow my slide into hell.

She tied my hands and feet together using her old nylon stockings and hit me with the yardstick, all the while scolding me for defying her, for not minding her, telling me she was doing this for my own good. I couldn't run. I couldn't move. I couldn't escape. Just like people captured by the Indians on TV.

I cried till I was breathless and gulping for air. Yet the beating continued.

When I thought the beating would not ever stop, she stopped. Shaking the yardstick at my face, she ordered me to stop crying. I kept crying. She threatened to hit me some more if I didn't stop crying. I hiccupped my way to a whimper. Rick and Beth stood by watching, silent and sober.

Then she untied me and made me drink the soup. There was a big lump in my throat, but I forced the soup past it. The illusion of the safety of our fort was shattered forever that day. We never played Fort again.

This story, like many difficult, painful experiences, revealed itself to me in pieces and parts over the years – like trying to look at something that is at a distance but there's a large tree or plant between you and it, and it's at night during a windy rainstorm, so you catch glimpses of parts of it at any given time. You see the easiest details first. As you battle your way through the storm, to move closer to that something, and when you finally get close enough to it, then the full picture is available for your viewing.

For many years, I "forgot" about this incident. Then, some time in my twenties or thirties during therapy, I remembered being tied up and beaten for refusing to drink the soup.

I told my sister Beth about it. She had forgotten it too, but when I reminded her of it, she remembered. For years, Beth would sometimes make a joke of it when we discussed our mother's ways and how it would be called child abuse today, ha, ha. Except I never found it to be very funny.

Now, another two decades or so later, I'm in this memoir writing class and as I focused on the few details I remembered, I was transported back to the full horrific experience. Not only had I shut away the pain of the beating, which was bad enough, but I had shut away the helplessness, humiliation, and complete subjugation of me by being tied up like an animal.

In that moment of catastrophe, I believe many decisions and conclusions were made by my three-year-old mind and heart. All my life I wondered why I didn't trust my mother, or why I always held back a piece of my heart. I don't have to wonder any more. Now I know why.

It's an amazing thing to recover the memory that influenced some very important life decisions. These decisions set me up in life, for better or for worse. Mostly for the worse, I believe.

What were some of those decisions and conclusions?

1. Playing Cowboys, Indians and The Fort was dangerous.
2. The Fort provided a false sense of safety. It did not protect me.
3. It's dangerous to say no.
4. I don't have the right to say no.
5. I will be made an example of and punished.
6. When someone hurts me, I cannot defend myself and no one else will either.
7. Mother cannot be trusted, especially when she says it's good for me.
8. I am defenseless against someone bigger and stronger.
9. I was so bad, I might as well be dead.

I believe that's the day I split from my inner being. I learned to keep many things to myself. I became a quiet child. If I had an opinion I kept it to myself mostly. I learned how to bury my opinions and feelings so deep, I wasn't aware of having opinions and feelings. It was safer this way.

I wish I could say that since the recovery of this memory, I've reconciled myself to it and I'm okay with all of it, but I can't. I'm still stunned by the enormity of the ramifications – like watching the ripples move in outward concentric circles when a stone is dropped into a lake, and trying to define the effect of the ripples on a distant shore.

I expect changes in my life from this, but it will not be simple. I suspect it will show up in a deepening knowledge and comfort with the person I already am, but I can't say for sure because I haven't gone down this road yet.

I want to be able to say something about having healed from this experience, or that I've forgiven and moved beyond this – but that would be coming out of my deep desire to make this story less ugly and more bearable.

I cringe at the ugliness of what was done to me that day.

I didn't want to live anymore that day.

I wish I could modify or make the story less horrible, but that would invalidate the truth of it. I want to face it and say, "It was ugly. It is ugly. I hate it. I hate what happened to me. I hate that it happened to me."

For my whole life I've asked myself if I loved my mother, and I've never been able to answer the question adequately. I've never been able to say 'yes' or 'no' clearly and succinctly. There has always been the heavy fog of disappointment, anger, sorrow, frustration, and hurt. For many years, I wondered what was wrong with me that I didn't love my mother in the way good children are supposed to. For years I thought there was something fundamentally wrong with me because I didn't trust or feel great love for her.

At least I don't have to feel guilty any longer for not feeling the warm fuzzies toward my mother. There was nothing wrong with me. I had a good reason and basis for that absence of trust.

I had always thought of forgiveness as holding the other

person blameless, but I always left myself out of the equation. What was I supposed to do with my feelings? Somehow I was supposed to "disappear" them, to swallow them, to "get over" them. But I could never manage to do that, so I couldn't consider that I could forgive, ever.

Now, I'm looking for a way to get through this and to the other side. I see and sense that it's the quality of my life that is at stake. I'm looking for a way to hold both the ugly, cruel memories of childhood and my profound caring for the deeply flawed human being I know as my mother.

❋

Here is what Francie had to say about this process of writing and sharing:

Through the process of writing and sharing my story, I am more of who I am, and more sure of myself. I know my mind and heart better, and am more comfortable with my feelings, even the uncomfortable ones. I am able to say the truth more readily. I know I've missed a sense of belonging and connection with others as a result of that event, but I realize that my work now is to belong to myself, by owning all of myself.

My life is a work in progress, as every life is.

Writing about sexuality can be a challenge for a writer. We worry about how much to reveal, and how to deal with shame or guilt. In this sparkling story, Kara captures the blushes and tingles of learning the "facts of life." This story won first prize in a contest sponsored by the California Writers Club, Sacramento branch. It has gone through many edits and revisions to find its way to this form.

Sex and the Sophomore
By Kara Jane Rollins

When we were released from fifth grade to go screaming to the playground, our favorite game was Reindeer. Girls dashed through the deep Wyoming snow with boys in mad pursuit. When a boy overtook a girl, he mashed her to the ground, and rolled all over her, leaving her covered with snow-prints and slush. What an honor to be chased and stomped. At age ten I believed mating was merely reindeer frolics.

By early adolescence I had acquired some vague notions about sex. Our family of eight girls kept the Kotex Company in business for years, so I knew about menstruation early. One day an older sister opened an industrial-sized Kotex box and exploded in laughter. The sanitary napkin machine had produced a defective pad, a yard-long piece of gauze containing two small wads of cotton a foot apart. She tied the thing on her head, positioning the cotton pads over her ears, and pranced into the living room where our father was reading a newspaper.

"Look, Dad. You get a free pair of earmuffs with each box."

"Yeah, honey," he said, not even looking up. He was an expert at tuning out the chaos of eight daughters.

In college a friend told me she had learned nothing about sex by age twelve and desperately searched the Bismarck, North Dakota library for a medical book. She was a Lutheran girl flooded with guilt, reading furtively the "reproduction" section, looking at illustrations of eggs and strange squiggly things attacking them. When an adult sat at her table she quickly hid the book. Her shame was so great she never went back, and spent a year puzzling over how in the heck the sperm got from one twin bed to the other. She devised two theories: (1) sperm wriggled snake-like through the air or (2) sperm and egg merged by osmosis. At least by age twelve I knew how pregnancy happened, but not much more.

The climax of my sex education came in 1957, my sophomore year in high school, when Miss Emily Gurchenko presented her notorious two-week sex education unit in gym class. Fifty-eight girls sat in a stuffy classroom between the boys' and girls' locker rooms, the air filled with the odor of wet towels and sweat socks. She barked, "Do not show the boys your sex education notebooks under any circumstances," as if the boys would take us hostage for them.

On the third day of class, Miss Gurchenko wheeled out enormous Merck Medical Instructional Charts, her biceps bulging under her black polo shirt with the whistle in the pocket. With thick, round pointer in fisted hand, she advanced on those charts ready to do battle. No one messed with Miss Gurchenko, a graduate of the Women's Army Corps.

She began with huge pastel diagrams of the male genitalia. A thirty-six-inch pink penis with mint-green testicles stared at me. As one of eight sisters, I had never seen such a thing. I didn't know if I should be looking or not and I was too paralyzed to take notes. She swung the pointer, whacking each colored portion of the diagram.

"The male has a special reproductive organ called the *penis*, which transfers sperm to the female. The long part of the *penis* is the *shaft*."

Whack. Whack went the stick.

"The cap-shaped top of the penis is called the *glans*, which is Latin for 'acorn.' "Sperm are not produced in the *penis*."

Whack. Whack.

"They are formed in the *testes*, two small, egg-shaped structures that hang below the main part of the body, in a loose bag of skin called the *scrotal sac* or *scrotum*."

Whack. Whack.

She rattled off anatomical terms as the stick flew in wide

arcs, smacking the charts so hard they teetered precariously. I thought she would break right through the paper.

Miss Gurchenko pivoted with a scowl on her face. "Any questions?"

The room was frozen in silence. Then Tangerine Withers raised her hand languidly, her finger nails painted coral to match her tight Jantzen outfit, her tongue playing at that little space between her front teeth. I was in awe of Tangerine, especially when she slowly undulated to the pencil sharpener in study hall, making sure all eyes were on her. I prayed to be that exotically hot someday. Tangerine's face was Dresden pale, her eyebrows plucked into tiny wings over thick mascara eyes. She wore tiny pearls in her pierced ears. Those were the days when we weren't allowed to pierce our ears lest we look like fallen women.

Miss Gurchenko laid down the stick and glared. "Yes? What's your question?"

"Oh, no," I murmured to myself, expecting an explosion from Gurchenko.

Heads swiveled toward Tangerine. Everyone knew she spent her lunch hour with her twelfth-grade boyfriend behind the Auto Shop Building. They had danced to *Earth Angel* at the sock hop, their hands roaming over each other. I suspected she had "done it" many times. Tangerine stuck out her chest and casually smoothed back her blonde ducktail, a tiny smile curving the corners of her mouth. Miss Gurchenko shifted her weight and cleared her throat. I couldn't move my body in my chair. The clock ticked loudly.

My mind pounded with questions that Tangerine *might* ask, things I secretly pondered. "How long does the penis stay erect? Can urine and semen come out at the same time? Do penises come in different shapes?" All I had seen were leaves or bunches of grapes on males in art books. And a final question... "Is the correct plural, *penises* or *peni*?" I was taking second year Latin.

Tangerine yawned nonchalantly and stretched. "I just wondered," she purred, "when do we get our report cards?" Her firm wide mouth was innocently pursed.

I scooted down in my seat, expecting some kind of atomic bomb. I couldn't believe Tangerine's audacity. Miss Gurchenko had told us we were supposed to be dead serious about this sex education stuff. She might kill her instantly, maybe with that stick.

The bell rang before Miss Gurchenko could react. We were out of there like cannon balls shot into the hallways of Billings Senior High School, our sex education notebooks pressed dutifully to our chests.

"Learn anything new?" Lanny Marino sneered at me as I stuffed my sex education notebook quickly into my locker. He was slouched up against the wall, his hair greased up high on his head, his black pants hanging low. He was wearing a pink and gray shirt with black buttons and a wicked smile that made my legs wobbly.

"Buzz off," I countered. "Wouldn't *you* like to know?" I slammed my locker shut and shuffled down the hall, holding my geometry book close, trying to keep my body from jiggling, acutely aware of his eyes on me. Boys sauntered by. I fixed my eyes above their waists, away from that "Mercky" area below the belt I had come to know that day and couldn't get out of my mind.

❋

Although Amy Peele's stories about spending the summer at her Aunt Mary's house were delightful, I felt that something was missing. Not wanting to delve into what might be painful secrets or memories that perhaps she didn't know she had, I gently questioned her about why those summers were so wonderful. Then she told me that she began writing her memoir with the idea that she would just write "the good stuff" and leave out the abuse and tension. The "dark side" was missing from her stories. We discussed what she wanted to do. Did she want to examine those stories? Did she feel that they were really part of her story? She decided to integrate some of the darker moments into the positive stories. Here is what she said about silencing the critic-censor:

Goldblatts
By Amy Peele

I find it difficult to write my memoir with all my critical siblings sitting on my shoulder constantly telling me I'm not accurate with my descriptions. Once I learned how to muffle or silence them, when the family audience was no longer in my head, I found the courage to write what I remembered and how I felt. It took me a while to do that.

Part of the challenge is describing how and what I felt without worrying about whose feelings I might hurt. Sometimes I wonder if certain family members should be dead before I submit my manuscript for publication. The writing stirs up some wonderful feelings and some sad, uncomfortable, and angry feelings that had been frozen inside and unavailable to me. After writing several stories, I learned to just see what feelings came up and deal with them as they thawed out. I do feel lighter after writing some stories. It's as if the story in my head held me hostage, but once I wrote it, it wasn't as big on paper as it was in my mind. I'm not sure that I will use all the stories I wrote, but I'm glad I wrote them. I'm also thankful for the psychological support of Linda Myers's memoir group and the encouragement to go for the hard stuff.

It was a cool fall Saturday morning in Park Forest, Illinois. The leaves had just started to turn red and orange with tips of yellow. I was ten and my sister Lorna was three years older. Lorna usually took me with her on her capers since our sister Charlene, the oldest girl, would never consider such things. I'd go along with whatever Lorna said or she'd beat me up.

"Amy and I are going down to the Plaza." That's all the information Lorna gave Charlene. She never was much for words, and she thought everyone should mind their own goddamn business. Charlene looked her square in the eye. "You two don't have any money to go shopping. What are you going to do there?"

Lorna said, "We can window shop, and you can't stop us!"

Charlene shook her head, ignoring her. Sometimes they would get into knock-down-drag-out fights, with hair pulling and lots of swear words. Lorna had been really angry since my dad left.

We crossed the front lawn that our brother John had just mowed. Blades of fresh-cut grass stuck to the sides of our sandals. The Plaza was two long blocks from our house, a huge collection of stores that circled a big white tower with a clock on top of it.

I said to Lorna, "Which store are we going to—Marshall Fields?" I loved their Barbie Doll clothes collection.

"You know we're too poor to walk into that place. We're going to Kresge's for some fries, and then I want to go over to Goldblatts to look around."

Sounded just fine to me. Kresge's was our five-and-dime and had the second-best soda counter at the Plaza; the first one was the Grill. We slid into the red booth, and the waitress with her frilly white apron and black short dress came up. "What do you girls want?"

Lorna took her baby-sitting money out of her pocket. "We'll have a large order of fries and a cherry coke."

"You both have to order something or you can't sit in a booth."

Lorna gave her one of her mean looks with her eyebrow up. "Then give her a cherry coke too."

"I want a vanilla coke."

The lady turned around and went to order. Lorna gave a loud sigh, "What a bitch." I cringed, hoping the lady didn't hear her and wouldn't throw us out. I wondered if she knew how poor we were. After we enjoyed every last crunchy fry with a dip of catsup, Lorna got up and nodded for me to follow her.

We went up and down different aisles looking at hair products, empty photo albums, cheap clothes, make-up, and then headed down to my favorite aisle, the candy aisle. Lorna grabbed my blouse and hissed, "Look, just pick one or two candy bars you want and quickly shove them down your shorts. Then we're getting the hell out of here."

I was scared, but I didn't have any money and I wanted some candy. I grabbed a five-cent Butterfinger and a few Reese's peanut butter cups and shoved them in my shorts. My heart was racing and my eyes were darting all over the place. I knew I was doing something wrong, but also it was exciting.

Lorna grabbed my arm. "Just look normal and slowly walk towards the door. Stop and look at something right by the door, then meander like you got all the time in the world."

Good thing she told me that or I would have run out the door and surely given myself away. A few stores past Kresge's, I went to take the candy from my pants, but Lorna said, "Not yet. Wait till we turn the corner, in case anyone's looking."

I had put the candy in the middle of the elastic band of my shorts. "They're digging into my skin."

"Shut up, you big baby, we're almost out of sight."

A few minutes later I was enjoying my Butterfinger. I opened the Reese's peanut butter cups and gave her one. We strolled past Fannie May Candies—that was for the really rich people. We passed the Holiday theater, and then walked into Goldblatts, the candy and wrappers long gone. I followed Lorna to the record area, and she started looking through the forty-fives. I knew she didn't have any money left, but I figured she was just browsing. Next thing I knew she took a stack of forty-fives and shoved them down the front of her pants, grabbed my arm, and started for the door. I shook my arm free and kept pace with her until we got right in front of the double doors to leave. I stopped.

Lorna gritted her teeth, "Amy, come on now, we have to go!"

"You go look around. I want to look at these wallets." I started picking up a black leather one. It was soft, with lots of room for pictures and a little clip coin purse attached to it.

She insisted, "We're leaving now!" I saw her red face, put down the wallet, and followed her outside.

As we started to walk towards Sears, a lady called after us, "Excuse me girls, could you please wait a minute?"

It was Marie, the store detective. Everyone knew her. She was a running joke. She was five-foot-two and wore a tan raincoat even when it wasn't raining. She wore old-lady black shoes and carried a black handbag that was almost as big as she was. You could spot her a mile away, but we hadn't.

She walked up to Lorna. "Young lady, do you have something that doesn't belong to you?"

Lorna was quick to reply, "No!"

"I think you do. Now, follow me back into the store, and I won't call the police. We can keep this as store business."

Lorna started to follow Marie back into the store, and I followed. My heart was pounding so loud I thought everyone could hear it. Marie took us behind a curtain marked "Employees Only" and into a small room with a gray metal desk. She closed the door.

"Now, what's under your shirt?"

Lorna took the records out and threw them on the desk. I couldn't believe she was acting like this. We were in serious trouble. Marie looked Lorna straight in the face. "How often do you two girls steal here?"

Lorna let out a huff. "We've never stolen anything here before."

"How can I believe you? If you steal, you probably lie too."

"Believe anything you want. I don't give a damn."

Marie was angry now. "That's it. I'm calling your parents, and I may even call the police. What's your name?"

Lorna calmly looked at Marie. "Carol Wright." I couldn't believe she was lying to Marie. We were getting in deeper by the minute.

"What's your phone number?"

"PI 8-7864."

Marie picked up the phone and dialed. A man's voice answered.

"Hello, this Marie from down at Goldblatts. I'm sorry to tell you we have your daughter Carol here for shoplifting." A pause.

Marie slammed down the phone. "He doesn't have a daughter!" She looked over at me. "Now you better tell me your real names or I'm calling the police to come pick you both up, and we'll see you in court."

Lorna was giving me the "don't spill it" look. I was only ten, and I wasn't good at lying or stealing yet. I blurted out, "My name is Amy Peele and this is my sister Lorna, and our number is PI 8-2434."

I could feel Lorna's eyes burning a hole through the side of my head. "Nice job, asshole."

Marie dialed our number, and my mom answered the phone. We were screwed.

"Mrs. Peele, this is Marie from Goldblatts. I'm sorry to have to call you like this, but we have your two daughters Lorna and Amy here. They've been caught shoplifting. I'd rather not call the police. Could you come down here so we can settle this matter here at the store?"

Marie put the receiver down, a look of confusion on her face. "I'm sorry, girls. Your mother wants me to go ahead and call the police."

I was shocked and scared as I watched Marie call the Park Forest police department. I looked over at Lorna for some comfort, but she was acting as if nothing was wrong. I think she had watched too many prison movies. It seemed like a long time until a uniformed policeman knocked on the door. Marie stepped outside and closed the door. Lorna leaned over and gave me a knuckle sandwich punch in my left arm, hard. She always made her middle finger knuckle stick out so it stung when she hit, and it always left a bruise on my arm.

"You stupid bitch, if you hadn't told her our name she might have let us go. Now we're really dead, thanks to you. Mom's gonna beat us."

The officer opened the door and gestured for us to follow him. I looked down at the floor as we walked out to the police car, hoping no one who knew us was in the store. It was already dark out, which meant it was dinnertime at our house. Our brothers and sisters would know about our crime.

The police station was a couple of blocks from the Plaza. We were taken into a big room with a wooden desk and chairs. A short, fat, balding officer with glasses sat across from us. His badge said "Officer Milky."

"Hello, Lorna and Amy. It seems we have a problem here."

How did he know our names already?

"You want to tell me what happened over at Goldblatts?"

I wasn't going to speak. I didn't want a bruise on my other arm. I nodded to Lorna.

"I stole a few forty-fives, big deal."

Officer Milky pulled his chair up to the table and leaned toward us. "It's a very big deal because both of you have a police record now. I've called your mother three times, and she has hung up on me each time. She says you got yourselves into this mess, you should get yourselves out. She wants me to keep you here. She doesn't want thieves in her house. I can't say I blame her."

He looked over at me. Tears were rolling down my face. This was the most terrible trouble I had ever gotten into in my life. "Amy, you're a little young to be in jail overnight, don't you think?" I nodded my head and then burst into a full-blown cry. Lorna sat there not reacting to Office Milky. He handed me the Kleenex box.

"I'll try your mother one more time, but if she doesn't come, then we're going to have to ship you to Juvenile Hall in Chicago Heights, and you'll spend the night there." He got up and went out of the room. I looked at Lorna, tears streaming down my face. "This is just great!"

She glanced at me, "Just shut up. They can't send us to Juvenile Hall. Our crime isn't that big."

Officer Milky came in shaking his head. "You two ladies are lucky. Your Mom's on her way, but I wouldn't want to be you two when you get home. She is very angry and tired. Too bad she has to work all day and then come home to this kind of news. Shame on both of you! Follow me."

Officer Milky motioned for us to sit on black vinyl chairs in the lobby, then went into the other room. "Stay there. Your mother will be here in a minute." As I turned my head I saw my mother, still dressed in her white nurse's uniform, walking into the police station. She walked right by us as if we didn't exist and around to speak to Officer Milky. She seemed to know her way around the station. She came back into where Lorna and I were sitting. "Get in the car."

We got up and she followed us. As soon as we left the parking lot she started in. "So, Lorna. You're not content getting into trouble alone. You have to bring your little sister along for the ride now. Amy, where is your common sense? You know better. Shame on both of you for disgracing yourself and our family. It's bad enough your father leaves me with six kids, debt, and no money, but then this shit. I work seven days a week, ten hours a day just to keep a roof over your heads and food on the table, and this is how you show me respect. Well, I've had it! Lorna, I've grounded you, taken away every privilege, and you still defy me. This is the last straw!"

She pulled into our driveway, slammed the car into park. "Both of you get inside and go straight to the bathroom." My mother went into the kitchen, took something out of a drawer, and headed toward the bathroom.

I was trembling. I didn't know what was going to happen. Lorna had long since detached from my mother's threats and beatings. It seemed as if nothing could make her feel remorse. The rest of the house was silent. We both went into the bathroom. My mother followed and closed the door. She placed big silver scissors on the sink. "Take off all your clothes. You want to act like criminals, I'm going to treat you that way!"

My mother's rage was intense, she was out of control.

She made my sister Lorna stand under the cold shower, and then she began to cut her long brown hair off in clumps. I screamed and screamed for her to stop. She kept cutting. I stood there shivering from fear and cold, scared that I was next and scared for my sister. Would my mother do something even worse to her?

It took a long time. I stood there listening to my sister scream and cry. My mother turned to me and said, "Next time you two think about stealing something, think of this. Now put your clothes back on, clean up this mess, and go to bed."

My expectations of what she was going to do to me lessened as I saw her enter her bedroom, but my fear of what might happen another day was still strong. I don't remember exactly what happened next, but I know I cried myself to sleep. None of us kids talked about what happened that night, just like we never talked about Dad leaving.

❈

In a class I was teaching, we all listened as Lea read this new story, enthralled by the child's voice. It demonstrated how a very young child's voice can bring such immediacy, showing a sense of wonder and awe, and a child's spirituality.

Twice Taken Unawares
by Lea DuRard

This story covers two turning points in my early years. I wrote it in two parts at separate times, and each part came quickly as I put myself back into my childhood perception. More difficult, and unexpectedly so, was sharing it aloud in class. About a third of the way through reading I began to feel for the first time the pain I had experienced as a child. Tears began to well up, and I had trouble reading on even though the story got lighter. But at the end I felt relief and gratitude for having found that child once more, and being witnessed by the class.

It wasn't every Sunday that "Momee," my grandmother, came to take me to church, but it happened often enough the year that Daddy got married to Pat and we moved out of Momee's house and I started Mrs. Smith's first grade. Daddy must have known how I missed living with my grandmother and encouraged her visits to cheer me up.

On the Sunday mornings she came I was so excited I almost burst. I'd choose a pretty dress to wear, and since Momee was old-fashioned and wore hats, I would put on my white beret with the gold stars just for her.

When she'd drive up I'd be at the living room window, dying to run to her, but Pat said I should always wait inside. Momee would walk, sometimes with a cane, in that slow way of hers up to the front porch. As soon as I'd fling open the front door and the screen, she'd bend down and wrap her arms around me. When I pressed into her soft wide bosom, she felt like heaven and Aunt Jemima rolled into one.

It always felt like holding my breath, waiting for all the living room hello's and goodbye's to be over, and then I'd practically whoop, grabbing onto Momee's long black dress as we went out into the warm morning air.

After we'd get in her gray Packard car, she'd fumble a little with the keys and set the air conditioning knobs just right. I'd slide in right next to her, relaxing into her world. She smelled like chalky bath powder and sweet honeysuckle all mixed together, and I loved it. And she had a soft neck with lots of creases to nuzzle into. So I'd cuddle close. She'd pat my shoulder, and off we'd go.

First Presbyterian was a big building sitting high on the only bluff in town. Back in the days I was going with Momee, I often went to the Sunday School room while she'd listen to the preacher in the sanctuary. But there were other times when she'd ask me to sit with her, and I was happy to be by her side. The last time I ever sat with her in the pew was different from all the rest, and after it Daddy never let her take me to church again.

It must have been a special Sunday that day—it was some time after Easter and the pews were all filled. I felt like the only kid at the big folks' service. We sat where she always sat, on the left side, near the aisle, half-way up. I liked it there, because I could see Pastor Dan high up in his box but he wasn't so close that he could really see me. Sometimes I'd bring Crayolas and color on the church bulletin; other times I'd fiddle with the little glass communion cups, switching them around in their little holes in the railing in front of me.

Or I'd thumb through the hymnal and practice my reading. I liked studying the titles of the songs, trying to figure out what they meant. "What a friend we have in Jesus" was one of my all time favorites because I knew the verses by heart and the song felt friendly.

But on that one Sunday Momee didn't have patience with my playing with the hymnal. She must have known what was coming, because she kept telling me to listen to the sermon. After it was over, Pastor Dan came down to stand in front of us all. The choir broke out singing something that wasn't listed on the hymn board, and I half buried my head in the hymnal, hoping to find the song. Momee all of a sudden was leaning way forward in the pew. The song was about "coming to the river" and I didn't know what page it was on but everybody around us was joining in. Momee turned to me and began squeezing my hand hard.

"Ow, that hurts," I said. Momee's brown eyes were very bright behind her glasses, and I could feel her look going right through me.

"I want you to go up there," she whispered.

"Why?"

"Because I said so," she snapped. Her tone said "no-nonsense" and got my hackles up.

"But why?"

"Because you need to be saved."

"Saved?" I searched through my mind, thinking maybe I had forgotten something I was supposed to know.

"Saved?" I asked again. "Saved from what?"

By then there was lots of commotion, with most everyone in the pews standing and singing, and some were swaying, and three or four grownups were walking down the aisle to the front.

"I want you to go up there NOW." There was a fierceness in Momee's voice as she pointed toward Pastor Dan.

"I don't want to," I said, beginning to feel scared. "I don't want to."

"Do you want to be damned, Lee Ann? Is that what you want?"

Her words stung, and I moved back from her like she was poison.

"Damned?" The word rolled around in my head. It was a cuss word I had heard, but I didn't know its meaning.

Then she reached over and shook me. "Do you want to live in hell like your mother?"

Something snapped inside me and everything went blank. For a moment there was no sound and I couldn't think. Then my ears had a ringing, and I could barely breathe. I tried to gulp fresh air and struggled until I pulled away from her. I turned my back on her, so that she couldn't see my hurt.

It was the very first time any one besides Daddy had said a word to me about my REAL mother, about the precious person I sometimes tried to imagine. And Daddy had only talked about her once, saying my mother had had me and loved me, and that she'd died and was gone, just like Momee's husband was dead and gone. The time Daddy had said these things, I could tell it made him very, very sad. I was afraid to tell him it made me sad too, because he would have felt even worse. So I just kept my feelings to myself and had no idea, all this time, that anyone else even remembered her.

Yet here Momee was, bringing up my mother from out of nowhere, and stomping on something very special and secret in my heart. Momee was mad at my mother or mad at me and talking about hell and I didn't know why. I could scarcely make out the words because my heart was thumping so hard and the church all of a sudden was so hot.

"Lee Ann, you listen to me," Momee's voice cut through me as she yanked me around to face her. She wiped at my eyes with her handkerchief and pulled me close. Then her tone changed.

"If you'll do as I say, I'll get you an ice cream."

"I don't want an ice cream. I want to go home."

"Don't you want to be a good girl? Don't you want to be Jesus's friend?"

I couldn't tell that minute if she was being mean or kind, I just knew we were in a tug of war over something big I didn't understand and didn't want to—didn't want to because it felt like something scary, like there was something fiery and forever at the bottom of it. All I wanted was to let go of the tug rope and run away.

And so I did. I jumped up and left Momee sitting right there in the pew and everyone singing as I shoved my way to the aisle and ran all the way to the back of the church and out to the parking lot where I slumped down next to some cars and wailed and wailed my heart out.

After that, Daddy took over driving me to Sunday School, and I let myself stop trying to think about what Momee had said about my mother not being in heaven because she was bad. It all was too big to understand, and it hurt, like when you're almost asleep and the wind slams a door shut and you feel the slam deep down in your back.

Daddy had said to forget Momee's words, that she'd gotten it wrong, that my mother was good, definitely very beautiful and very good. My mother had just gotten mixed up somehow, and when I got older he'd explain more if I asked him to. He was very sure she was in heaven, up there with Daddy's own father.

So I quit trying to make sense of anything but the God part. God loved everybody so that meant he loved my mother. And that made me want to know him better. Most nights I'd practically bury myself in the "Children's Illustrated Bible" that I got as a prize for reading better than first-grade level.

I liked the stories a lot. My favorites were about Noah's huge ark, and Joseph's coat of many colors, and Jesus as a boy teaching in the temple. Since the stories were about people who loved God and did what he said, I wondered what God had to say to me. So I prayed a lot, asking God to talk to me and to get me out of having to call Pat "Mom" like she wanted, because she wasn't. I prayed for my real mother too, and asked that she be up in heaven and that she remember who I was.

One evening something happened. I never told anyone because they'd think I just made it up or that I was crazy. It happened when I went to the school playground with a lot of older kids from the neighborhood. It was that cool time when it's still too light for fireflies but the air has a fresh feel that says it'll be getting dark soon.

The other kids took over the baseball diamond, but I wanted to be on the merry-go-round. It was wobbly as always, and there was no one else to push with me but that was okay. I sat on it backwards and stretched out on my back with my hands holding the metal rings and my feet sticking straight out. Every once in awhile I let my feet drop to give myself a push. I went round and round but real slow, just taking my time.

I got to really looking at the sky. It was grape-colored with pink and blue, like a rainbow popsicle, and it was huge. I started wondering if heaven was as big, and the more I stared at the sky the more I thought heaven couldn't be, because this sky was so big it was "infinite," which Mrs. Smith had told us in school meant endless. Forever.

Each time I rode around, the closer the sky came.

And suddenly all at once the sky started opening up, bigger and bigger and wider and wider, like it was going to swallow me, except I wasn't scared at all. And I wasn't thinking about God or the sky, I WAS the sky, and the sky was heaven and it was God, and I was melting into it and floating, and everything kept opening and opening.

I was happy and warm and safe in that space because somehow I just knew something wasn't ever going to let me fall. It was infinite in there for sure, and very quiet. There weren't any stars, just lots and lots of space that was part of me and I was part of it and all of it was God.

I lay there on my back, so peaceful floating I had no idea what time it was. When some of the kids came over and said it was time to go, I wondered if maybe I looked different, if anyone could see from my face that I'd been somewhere special, but no one really looked at me at all. I went home feeling quiet inside and happy, knowing in my heart of hearts that God would take care of both me and my mother.

❄

Imagining the Past
By Sarah Weinberg

There is no way to process the grief and loss passed from one generation to the next not only in the not knowing but in the imagining of what might have happened. Ma used to speak about her grandfather, a rabbi in Russia, who never emigrated to America. My Aunt Lillie says his son Sam tried to find him by contacting the Red Cross, but Uncle Sam had no luck. We don't even know his name.

Some questions have haunted me over the years. Why did my grandmother Esther Annie travel alone to America? Did my great-grandfather plan to join his daughter in America later? Was he too poor or too old to come? Did his responsibilities as a rabbi keep him there?

Since a cloud of gloom is in the air whenever Ma mentions him, I decide to conjure up his presence, waiting for an answer and the secret of our family's past to be unraveled.

In the voice of my maternal great-grandfather: I live in Belarussia, in a town called Bobruisk. The weather is cold here so I often put on my black fur hat to keep the edges of my ears warm. I have boots on with leather soles to protect myself from the cold and snow. I am proud to own a pair of boots with no holes. I have a long gray beard that keeps me warm and *pehas*, long locks that come down in front of my ears, which have never been cut. I wear a black suit and a long topcoat.

My prayer book is my daily companion. I take it with me wherever I go. When a question lies heavy on my heart, I open my prayer book randomly and I lay my finger anywhere on the page for the answer.

My prayer book was given to me by my grandfather on the Sabbath of my bar mitzvah. The pages are worn and yellowed with age and daily fingering. I open it to follow the three daily services. And I just start chanting and reading the Hebrew, with my body swaying back and forth and from side to side.

I pray for my children's safety. I had four of them—two daughters and two sons. One of my sons was a published

Russian poet who died of pneumonia, and so did my wife. This *Pesach* I say the *Kaddish* to honor their memory and elevate their souls. The first few words of the Kaddish prayer—*yitgadol*, will be made great; *yitkadash*, will be made holy; and *sh'meh rabah*, the name of the great one—inspired my faith in G-d.

When I say the Kaddish, I see my wife's face, the softness in her eyes, and the corner of her lips curled up in a smile. My son, he had such broad shoulders and always stood proud, with his chin up. He branched away from religious studies and acquired a general education. He had a love of literature and an interest in politics. His poetry showed his gentleness and sensitivity, describing the richness of Jewish cultural life in Bobruisk and creating an ideal society. I miss them.

There is no public place for me to lead services since the fire of 1902. Fifteen temples were destroyed, including my own. Over two thousand Jewish families lost their homes, and some of the congregants in my own temple died. It was a surprise when the Czar came to town donating rubles to rebuild Bobruisk.

Now we meet in my home or other people's homes. We must form a *minyan*, a prayer group of ten or more men, for prayers like the Kaddish to be said out loud. In the morning when I pray, I wrap myself up in my *tallit*, a prayer shawl, a safe cocoon for me to disappear into. The *tzit tzit* dangles around me as I move in prayer; it is a fringe on the outer corners of the prayer shawl, with open threads that are not hemmed in and closed.

In biblical and post-biblical times in Israel, the edges of the fields were left unharvested by the owners for the poor. The tzit tzit at each corner reminds me of the corners of the fields left for the poor. The boundaries and borders are fuzzy, not clearly defined, which shows me that we are not separate beings, we are all interconnected.

It is dangerous here; there are rumors of pogroms coming to our town. Pogroms have already happened in many other Russian cities, such as Kisheniev, Zhitomir, and Retshitse. One could come like a lightning bolt at any moment. The Cossacks ride into towns with their brightly colored uniforms and their magnificent horses. Their hooves make the boom boom sound of a fierce and powerful drum. The Cossacks come to slaughter people, especially us Jews, for our religious beliefs. I want my children to have a better life. This is no place for a Jew. I have booked passage to the New World for my three remaining children. My son Sam and my oldest daughter have made it over there, but I keep my youngest daughter, Esther Annie, with me. I used to hide my baby in the large stove oven as part of a safety drill when Cossacks were expected in our town because I heard many stories about them raping girls. Esther Annie is a teenager now, and she is too big to hide in the stove.

Last week I booked passage for Esther Annie to leave. I am an old, sick man. I don't have the money to join my children in America.

The morning of Esther's departure I put on my *tefillin*, the two small leather boxes containing Torah passages written on parchment. I wind the leather bands with the boxes, one on my forehead, the other leather box tied to my arm. I make the Hebrew letter *shin*, which stands for G-d's name, on my hand with the leather straps. I have carried out this ritual each day of my adult life, yet on the day Esther is to leave my hand trembles, and my arm flinches as I bind myself to G-d.

As I hug Esther Annie, my baby girl, and bid her farewell tears start to run down her face and mine. My mouth tastes their saltiness on my lips. I can still hear Esther's voice as she is leaving. "Daddy," she says, "please don't make me go."

She is my little girl, yet I force her to go. I wave good-bye from a distance. Tears hang in droplets on my beard. My hat falls off my head as I watch her go. I step on it accidentally and crush it to the ground. My heart tightens up in a knot. What if Esther doesn't make it to the New World, and I cannot join my children? Esther, my baby girl and my hidden delight. *Estar*, her Hebrew name, means "hidden." I hope she stays hidden and true to her namesake until she makes it safely to the New World. I hope she reveals who and what she is, and is able to shine on her own.

I have sent Esther to live with my cousins in a place far away called New York. I hope they treat her well. My son Sam and my oldest daughter went to live with relatives in Chicago. May G-d bless them and protect them. May G-d shine light upon their paths and grace them with peace.

Afterthoughts: It is indeed a courageous act to send one's children away. Now I understand the choice. There is a kind of knowing in Hebrew called *yadati*, which means "I know," in the soul and heart. By becoming my great-grandfather, yadati—I know in my soul and heart the pain of my ancestor. My grandmother Esther Annie Slobodin was born in 1888 in Bobriusk, Belarussia. She died when she was seventy years old in New York City on May 7, 1958, the year of my birth. How I wish I'd had the opportunity to know her!

I have a photograph of her sitting on a large, solid, wood chair next to my grandfather, who rests at her side on a wooden rocker. Grandpa's shoulder touches hers as his body slants toward her. She does not lean into him quite as much, although her head tilts very slightly in his direction.

A part of my heritage is my Russian Jewish ancestry. When I wrote this story it made the feeling of connection stronger. I did research on life in Bobruisk during the time my great-grandfather lived there. I had a feeling that he wore *pehas*, as is customary for Hassidic Jews, yet I did not want to leave this detail in the story until I knew it was historically accurate. I was delighted to learn about the Hassidic and Yiddish-speaking Jewish communities in Bobruisk. When I conjure up my great-grandfather's presence I believe that he wore *pehas*!

I know there were pogroms in Russia. I needed to research the time frames in which they occurred to be sure the information shared in my family while I was growing up was accurate. I found out that while pogroms took place throughout the 1880s, 1890s, and early 1900s, the pogrom wave actually avoided Bobruisk because of a strong resistance movement and the fact that it was a fortress town and a base for the Russian army. The wave that flooded many cities and villages in Pale of Settlement destroyed the mood in Bobruisk, where anti-Semitism was widespread and Jews were restricted from holding certain occupations. Some Jews were rich, but many who were poor left the city in droves. And there was genuine fear about the pogroms.

In order to see my relatives living out their lives and feel connected to them, I needed to learn about everyday life in Bobruisk, what type of a town it was, and its history. Through doing the research about my past and my roots to write this story, I experienced a sense of completeness that I had never known before.

❊

Allene has been in my classes for several years, where we all enjoy her quirky and creative way with words. As you can see here, her sense of humor is present even in a piece that has elements of seriousness—an artful weaving indeed about the imperfections and ironies that are a part of life.

Meds and Memoirs
By Allene Hickox

By the time I got to my psychiatrist's office, I felt happy and had lots of energy. I'd been taking Prozac for about a year now, gradually increasing my dosage from ten milligrams to twenty milligrams and recently to thirty milligrams a day – not a very big dose, I've been told.

I've been toying with writing something called "Is It the Prozac or the Prose?" Yes, words, written words, can have a healing effect on one's life. Hey, this isn't my idea. People have done research, such as James Pennebaker in Austin, Texas. He found that writing one's memoir helped to heal a person. And the memoir writing did not have to be about some dreadful trauma or only about jolly happenings. Either way worked.

So I began my journey along the path called, "This way to healing by writing your memoir."

Hey, I'm a really together person. What on earth about me needed healing? You guessed it: depression. Not just situational depression where the dog ran away or your favorite uncle died, but clinical depression, meaning your brain chemistry needs help to function as it should so you won't feel so depressed.

And that's where Prozac entered the door. Oh, I went to individual psychotherapy sessions, approximately five or six times. You see, I have Kaiser health insurance, and they really believe in brief therapy. Any briefer and I'd need a photograph of my therapist to remember what she looked like.

Yes, I'm able to override the stigma of mental disorder and the toxic shame of taking an antidepressant.

Being a "perfect patient," as my supervisor at work told me, I was compliant enough to join Kaiser's depression group. Do you realize how depressing it is to be in a group with only depressed people? I know we're all "more that our diagnosis," but really.

So I leave you this question, since I'm a lot less depressed in this past year, was it the medication or the memoir writing classes I've been enrolled in for the last year with Linda Joy Myers? I really believe these classes have dramatically contributed to my depression reduction.

I plan to keep on writing and writing and writing, okay? Where else can I find a group of memoir writers, and our teacher, willing to hang, really hang, on my every spoken word when I read what I've written? It's unconditional positive regard to the max. Eat your heart out, Carl Rogers.

Was it the prose or the Prozac? I'll leave the answer to you, dear listener.

❋

Appendix A

Meditations on Memory: Affirmations to Heal the Inner Critic

*W*e memoirists find ourselves in a special position as writers. In order to write a memoir, we must draw material from vague memories that can't be proved and are nearly impossible to research. We often wish we could remember the past with more clarity, but find it hard to get past certain barriers. The inner critic, the voice that derides our writing and even our ability to remember, contributes to procrastination with our writing, and gets in the way of capturing our memory stories. Meditation and relaxation can help us let down barriers to the deeper parts of ourselves and provide access to the gems of story that are buried there.

Entering the realm of memory requires us to leave current time and tune into a world removed from the present as we enter a state of deep awareness and inner listening. In this contemplative state, we can listen to the quiet stream of wisdom beneath our everyday consciousness.

This series of Memoir Mediations are designed to help you relax your body and your mind so you can remember more specifics about the past and become more open to your inner wisdom.

The inner critic, as well as the voices of society and family, can make our memories less accessible and block us from remembering things that are in conflict with the "official" story. The inner critic silences the more complex levels of truth. These contemplative exercises will ease the constant harangue of self-criticism and allow you to discover what stories from your life you want and need to write.

Writing can be done in a safe, welcoming way when we learn to manage the negative voices and worries that may arise when we delve into memory. These inner voices, often based on things that real people have actually said, may be painful, shameful, confusing, or blaming. It is important to have a method for dealing with these impediments to your writing, and to begin to forge a path back to claiming your voice with passion and clarity.

A Mini-Retreat

Taking time to relax and get away from regular life before you write is like having a retreat in your own home, garden, or meditation room. Writing is an act of courage and inner listening, akin to prayer, in which there is both a desire to receive inspiration and a suspension of conscious will. This exercise will relax your mind and body, making you more receptive to layers of memory.

Turn off your phones, and get away from the computer and the Internet for an hour. You may want to enhance your space with candles or aromatherapy. However, all you really need for this meditation is a comfortable chair and the willingness to take some time for yourself.

Relaxation and Visualization

1. Getting Relaxed

Select a chair with proper back support in which you can sit comfortably. Rest your feet on the floor and place your hands palms up in your lap. Inhale slowly while you count to four, then exhale counting to four. Take these breaths with the idea of letting go of the tension in your shoulders, your abdomen, and the muscles in your whole body. Even if your mind is still busy chattering with daily concerns, do your best to focus on the feeling of your breath in your body. In, out, relax. Let go, and sink into the chair.

Warmth and Heaviness—muscle relaxation
Repeat to yourself, "My feet are warm and heavy" three times, slowly. This phrase mentally instructs specific body parts to become relaxed and free of muscle tension. "My feet are warm and heavy; my calves are warm and heavy."

Breathe slowly, in and out, saying to yourself. "My legs are warm and heavy. I am breathing in a calm relaxed way, letting go of everything that worries me. My thighs are warm and heavy." Repeat each phrase three times. Keep your breathing slow and steady and deep.

Continue focusing on small areas of your body. "My hips… my lower back… my upper back...my shoulders are warm and heavy." Fill in the rest of the phrase and repeat each one three times.

When you notice an area that is resistant to becoming relaxed, spend more time taking deep breaths to open up the area of tension. Let the breath go, imagining tension sweeping out of your body and into the floor beneath your feet, all the way into the earth. These are called cleansing breaths, and they help you to deepen the relaxation. The face and head tend to carry extra tension, so it is important to spend time letting go of it.

"My scalp is heavy and warm, my eyes, my lips are relaxed, my cheeks are warm and relaxed." Repeat each phrase three times and end your focus on each part of your body with a cleansing breath.

Most people have tense shoulder muscles, as if we carry the burdens of our lives on our shoulders. Spend extra time talking to your shoulders: "My shoulders are warm and heavy. My muscles are loosening and letting go. I'm letting go of the weight of my feelings and responsibilities." Allow yourself to sink into this relaxation.

Now bring your attention to the front of your body. Each of us greets the world with the front of our bodies, a vulnerable and unprotected area. Our stomach and abdomen muscles grow tense with emotions and stress. We need to consciously let go of that tightness, and become willing to let our stomachs hang loose.

Repeat each phrase three times to yourself, pausing between each one. "My stomach is warm and heavy, my abdomen is warm and heavy. My muscles are loose and relaxed."

Allow your pelvis to hang loose and your stomach muscles to relax completely. Forget about the admonitions to hold your stomach in. No one is watching!

If your mind wanders, simply bring it back and re-focus on relaxing your muscles. "My stomach is warm and heavy. I am letting go of all the tension in my stomach, abdomen, and hips."

Scan your entire body in this fashion, from your head to your feet, repeating each phrase three times, feeling the warmth increase in each muscle set. Return to any areas that still seem tense, and end with a cleansing breath.

Check out your whole body. Notice which areas need more relaxation and bring your attention to them. Return to creating warmth and heaviness for any areas that are still holding any tension.

2. White and Golden Light Relaxation

White light is purifying and intense, golden light is healing and mellower. Use your intuition to sense which intensity of light you prefer to bring into your body.

Imagine a beam of white or golden light coming into the top of your head from above. Feel it as a comforting warmth splashing down from above, spilling over your head, bringing with it a sense of well-being, comfort, and deep peace. Feel your scalp, face, and neck deepen into a relaxed state. With each in-breath, invite in more light. With each out breath, let go of darkness, tension, and worry. Take steady breaths, bringing the light into specific parts of your body—shoulders, arms, ribs, stomach, and abdomen. Bring the light through your pelvis, across your hips and lower back. Fill your body with light.

3. The Elevator Technique

In a state of relaxation, we imagine ourselves on an elevator that allows us to choose how far to deepen our meditation. If you don't like elevators, imagine yourself floating up and down, with wings. We begin at floor one and imagine descending in the elevator to deeper and deeper states of relaxation, where our minds are open to whatever memories come up. If you are concerned about negative memories coming up during a meditation, imagine getting into the elevator to rise back up to the current time level.

In present time now, the elevator is on the ground floor, level one. The elevator you enter is large and friendly. This elevator will take you down into layers of memory and you always have complete control over it.

When you get into the elevator, repeat, "I am going down, deeper into my mind, deeper into my memories. Each level of the elevator takes me deeper and opens my mind more fully to my past. I am able at any time to stop the meditation."

Imagine the elevator going down from level one to level two, three, down to ten.

When you open the elevator door you emerge into your favorite landscape, where you feel completely safe. Some people imagine a beach with warm sand, others a hammock in the back yard, or a mountain meadow. Settle down into a comfortable position where you can relax to the images and memories that emerge.

If you feel unsafe or too uncomfortable, simply imagine getting up and taking the elevator to level one. Count to three and open your eyes. At any time you can open your eyes and be in the present.

Childhood Memories

Some people feel that they only have a few memories from childhood. Others worry about the reliability of memory. Impressions of the past have left their mark on us, whether positive or negative, which offer material for our stories. Sometimes we need to bypass the critic or the inner censor that keeps us from remembering.

Here, in a relaxed state, you can see what arises, gently and without forcing. Perhaps a memory arises as if in a dream, or a scene passes across your mind. You may ask yourself if it is "really" a memory. For now, it doesn't matter. You can decide later what to keep and what to discard from anything that comes up during a meditation or remembering exercise. To prepare for the child meditation, choose photos from a time you want to remember. Put the photos around you, noticing the details. Notice how you looked physically and think about how you felt at that age.

Relax into your favorite childhood place after doing the initial relaxation exercise. Where did you play? How were meal times and what were your favorite foods? What was it like to be in your family? Who were your mother and father? Allow your mind to venture into your earliest recollections—toys, pets, the sensuality of the world on your skin. The things that confused and delighted you about your world.

Look at your body at the age of one, three, or six. How did you feel about your physical self? Were you awkward or graceful, delicate or strong? What were your favorite activities? Who were your friends? What games did you play?

Often young children have a sense of spirituality. What did you think about God, heaven, or hell? Did you receive religious instruction—where and when? What is your strongest memory of church, synagogue? What is the first time you felt a sense of awe and wonder?

For young children, spirituality is often connected with awe, wonder, nature, and a sense of magic. Think about these special times and allow the memory of them to be full and rich inside your memory meditation.

Most people do not have perfect families and childhood experiences. You may have memories that you are not sure about, or you vaguely don't want to remember. Allow the relaxation to guide you into a felt sense in your body for what is right for you. If you enter into memories that are too disturbing, just take the elevator back up to level one and enter current time. Take a deep breath and open your eyes.

In your relaxed state, see and feel yourself in your body, for example, when you were six years old. The following is an example of how to deepen the experience of yourself at that age or another age as a way of eliciting memories.

Before you begin, think about your childhood body in the present tense. How long are your arms and legs? How do you feel in your body? Do you like yourself? Who do you most resemble in your family? Who are you closest to, and why? What details do you notice in your world?

Think of this meditation as a way of focusing completely, as if with a memory magnifying glass, on the small details in your life. When the meditation feels complete enough for you to begin, freewrite without stopping or censoring the details that you noticed. Have pen and paper handy, or your computer if you prefer, ready to let your fingers fly over the keys, staying as much as you can in that half-light of memory of another time and place.

Think about the sensual details that make up our world, the smells, sounds, feeling of a place and time. How does your skin and body feel? How does the world appear?

Examples of sensual detail:

"The land around me is huge, the colors are green, all kinds of green, bright white houses painted here and there, so bright I have to shade my eyes. Huge trees seem to talk when the wind blows."

"I am in my house which is big and has dark corners. I remember my favorite hide-out, the smell of laundry when mother folds it…"

"When I am six, I am smaller than anyone else. I see belt buckles and my grandmother's apron."

"The house smells of mother's perfume and the soup that Grandma makes, and Daddy's pipe."

The following is an example of stream of consciousness writing after a few minutes of meditation on childhood and the sensory details of memory.

"I am six years old. I am the smallest person in my family. Sometimes my skin feels so soft; I like rubbing the hairs along my arm. When Mommy is angry, I want to curl up and have her hold me. I want to see her smooth, happy face come back. Her frown makes me scared, and I start to shake.

"The best part is playing with my trains and dolls. It's my brother Jake's train, but he is nice, some of the time and lets me play with it. I love the cool metal and the way the wheels move. I love the smell of the living room and the smell of soup on the stove when Grandma comes. She is big and wide, wears big shoes and she stomps, clunk, clunk when she walks. Her apron is always a little dirty where she wipes her hands, but she makes me feel special. My heart hurts when she is gone.

"The things that make me scared are thunderstorms, and the big dog on the corner, and the creak of a door. I think I see ghosts sometimes. I don't like it when Mommy and Daddy go into their room and shut the door, or when Jake teases me and leaves me out of his games. I don't like it when Mommy spanks me and I hate it when she doesn't smile at me. The best part is when she is happy with me again, and I love the feel of her warm body next to me, and the forehead without its creases. Her eyes tell me everything."

History of your life: Family Photos

Get out the family album to look at the photos of your parents when they were young, or your grandparents, aunts, and uncles. Notice your visceral reactions when you look at the photos and how you feel about the people pictured.

What do you know about the times in which they lived? What stories from the past influence the family, and you, in the present?

In your relaxed state, muse over the photos. Your imagination is one of the most useful tools in creating stories. Select a photo that draws you in, that tickles your curiosity. Begin to write your questions about the photo and what you think is going on. For instance, I have a photo of my grandfather holding my mother when she was a baby. His face is youthful, his jaw lean, and his hands are huge as they support her head. In the background is a wicker baby buggy. My mother is a six-month-old infant, and I know from the family history that already there is trouble between her parents.

As I look at the photo, I wonder what happened between my grandmother and grandfather on the day of the photo. Did they have a fight that led up to their separation? Did my mother nurse or have a bottle? How much did she cry and what were her dreams? What seeds were being sown on that day that led to later troubles? Why were they taking photos of her that day? Who took the picture? What happened afterward?

I can only speculate about what happened so long ago, but the photo stimulated me to write about my mother, whom I didn't know very well, as a little girl with whom I could identify as I thought about her young life. This process of imagination and compassion helped me to forgive her as she was dying. She had been an abandoned little girl, like me.

In thinking about your own family history, consider the questions you may have about your family. What happens when you think of parents and grandparents as small children? Notice where your mind and your imagination want to go and what they hold on to. These images are useful seeds for stories.

Spirituality Meditation

When holding a newborn baby only a few minutes old, we are drawn to the deep, wise look in the baby's eyes. Where was that soul before arriving on earth? Some mothers talk about babies being wise beyond their years when they hear remarks their children make about God, heaven, angels, and various spiritual ideas. The parents wonder if the child remembers the soul's journey to this earthly realm.

When my students share about their childhood reflections, they remember early spiritual experiences in the wildness of nature, among trees, with pets, or looking at the stars. Mountains, streams, the silence of snow on a winter day. Most children are fascinated by the natural world around them and feel drawn to exploring it. Small, everyday things are major explorations for children. They are more psychologically open to receiving the world with a sense of wonder and awe. In your meditative state now, you may begin to remember moments when you were amazed, and sensed that you were part of something much larger than yourself.

Allow yourself to linger in these memories. See where they take you, what images, sensations, feelings arise. Linger in the moments you felt were spiritual—however you define that word.

• What was your first spiritual experience? Where were you? How old were you?

• How did you feel about:

  • God;

  • Heaven, hell, and the afterlife; Jesus, Buddha, Mohammed, saints, rabbis and other spiritual figures;

  • The leaders of your church or Sunday School;

  • The Bible, Koran, Torah, or other spiritual teachings;

  • reincarnation.

• What spiritual thoughts and images would comfort you when you were a child?

• Did you have positive and negative feelings about spirituality?

• Did you have a sense of awe, fear, peace, or comfort as you considered your spiritual questions?

• How and when did you have these feelings?

• How did your spiritual feelings affect your life?

• What life decisions did you make based on your spiritual experiences and feelings?

• How did your spirituality change over your life? Think about each decade of your life and what new events, experiences, and knowledge affected these changes

• Allow your mind to venture into other questions, images, and memories you feel are important to your spirituality. Give yourself time to explore these thoughts and memories, and notice your emotions.

Freewrite

When you are ready, do a freewrite about what you notice, see, feel, hear, or sense from your meditation. Let the words flow from your pen without censoring, and remain willing to receive what comes.

There are many definitions of spirituality. Write your own definition. Write about what your spiritual experiences were from the earliest age you remember. Think about the direction and path your life has taken.

There might be more spiritually oriented questions that arise, as this subject is very significant in many people's lives. Most spiritual teachers talk about dark nights of the soul, when everything seems hopeless and hurtful. Yet such moments may whisper about new beginnings or possibilities that are revealed through the crisis.

• When and where were the darker moments, and what did you learn from them?

• How did the paths you didn't take shape where you are now?

• How did you wrestle with the dark and light moments in your life?

• What spiritual teachers and mentors have helped you in your life?

• What spiritual philosophy do you have now?

Inner Critic

The Inner Critic—everyone is familiar with it. It's the voice that silences you. It undermines your confidence in facing the blank page, and speaks to your doubts and the part of you that fears writing your stories down, expressing yourself, and having your full voice. The clever critical voice can be nasty, telling you such things as:

• Your story doesn't matter.

• Your life is not that interesting.

• No one would care about my little stories.

• My family will be mad if I write this.

• How do I know what I'm writing is a real memory?

• My writing is so bad.

- No one will want to read this.

- How do I know what the truth is?

- I'm not a real writer.

In a relaxed state, make a list of what the inner critic says. Allow this inner voice to speak freely, keeping your pen and paper nearby. The more you know about what the critic says that stops you from writing, the more you will be able to counteract its effect.

Affirmations

Affirmations are positive thoughts and feelings that counter the doubts and negative voices in our heads. Affirmations are a positive, healing, and comforting way of bringing balance into our minds and hearts.

The following affirmations will help to counteract the negative voices of the inner critic. Once you understand how an affirmation works as a counteractive voice, you can create your own specific affirmations that balance the specific voices of your own inner critic.

Enter your safe place of relaxation, knowing that you bring with you the burden of your inner critic. Feel this burden on your shoulders and all the places in your body where you are tense with the fears and worries your critic brings.

Rest into your safe place in a relaxed position. Allow each voice to come to your consciousness, holding it while you repeat to yourself, "I have a right to write my story. My voice matters. What I think and feel is important."

Such self-affirming comments help balance out the minimization that occurs with the inner critic.

Repeat each affirmation three times while you bring the golden light into your body, noticing places where you are tense and tight, where you feel any kind of block. Ask your muscles to relax to let go of the critic's power over you. Repeat, "My muscles are warm and heavy, and I am letting go of the critic voice. I am creating new affirmations to use each time I feel my resolve to write slipping."

Below is a list of affirmations to counteract the inner critic. Make up your own to fit your critic specifically.

• My life is unique and I want to share my wisdom.

• My stories are important to me, affirming who I am.

• I will not share my writing self with anyone who might criticize me.

• Publishing is not the goal of my first draft, so I will write just as I wish.

• I can't prove my memories so I will write what I remember and not worry about it.

• I give myself permission to write.

• If memories I don't like arise, I can write something else.

• I will breathe into love and acceptance as I write.

• Each time I write is a stepping stone to freedom

• When I write the truth, I balance my world.

• My family is not reading this while I write.

• I will not let my critic stop me.

• My life is important, and my thoughts and experiences matter.

Take a cleansing breath, allowing your affirmations to create a sense of strength and confidence in your body.

Fear, Shame, and the Dark Past

The reaction of family and loved ones, and family dynamics that label our writing as disloyal or wrong, keep many people from writing their truths. Often the writer is overwhelmed with fear and shame, and feels that she must remain silent.

The inner voices that haunt many of us say things like:

• You can't write that, it would hurt (your mother, father, aunt, uncle, grandmother, etc. insert name here).

• My siblings and relatives won't agree with my truth.

• I am afraid of being rejected by my family if I write my truth.

• I can't write what really happened—it's too embarrassing.

• My family always wants to know what I'm writing—so if I don't write, then I don't have to deal with them.

• I feel shame and guilt when I write.

• I feel angry when I write.

• I feel helpless and little when I write.

• The past is too overwhelming and shameful.

• The past is too dark and nothing good happened.

Breathing deeply, invite white and golden light into your mind and body as these fears/worries/negative voices arise. Listen to your own voices, and write down what they say. Pay attention to each one, then counter it with reassurance and comfort, such as:

• You don't have to write anything that disturbs you.

• What you write remains private and contained. No one needs to hear it. You don't have to share your work for now, or even talk about the fact that you write.

Suggestions to complete your meditations and affirmations

If the dark past is demanding your attention, write for a brief period, then put your work away. It is more intense to write in present tense. If you want to put the past farther away, use third person (he/she) and past tense.

Finish your writing sessions with a white and golden light meditation. Write positive stories to balance the darkness. The more you work with the inner critic, and keep writing anyway, the more freedom you will find. Your self-esteem will increase, and you will feel emotionally stronger.

You may want to work with one critic voice, paired with one affirmation. Try to keep your time with these meditations simple and welcoming. If at any time you become uncomfortable and feel that the journey into the past is too much, you may choose to stop the meditation and do something nurturing in present time. Leave the memories alone until you feel ready to deal with them.

If you are in therapy, you might bring these experiences to the attention of your therapist. If you feel tight and stiff places in your body, you might consider holistic approaches to healing, such as massage, acupuncture, and chiropractic work. There are a variety of healing approaches that integrate mind and body.

Take good care of yourself, as a person and as a writer.

Note: Author suggests these meditations as a means to get in touch with layers of memory and to come to the writing with a more relaxed attitude. However, if you are concerned about unpleasant memories coming up, or don't feel comfortable in a deeply relaxed state, the exercises may not be best for you. The author is not responsible for any results incurred by the reader who uses these exercises. They are suggestions for relaxation only, with no promises for specific results.

Appendix B

Developmental Questionnaire

*7*hese questions are meant to stimulate memories about your life chronologically. Think about them; write about them in your journal. They may lead to stories. If a question upsets you, move on to another one. Or you might choose to write about whatever bothered you for 15 or 20 minutes, a short writing exercise to facilitate healing. You can come back to any question at any time. You do not have to go through the questionnaire chronologically if you don't want to. If a subject grabs your interest, and you find yourself with strong memories or images, then start writing. Use the questions as guides to help you remember and think about what needs healing in your life and what scenes and memories are a part of you.

Keep in mind that at different stages a child is psychologically prepared in different ways to handle the stresses of life. If a situation appropriate for a sixteen year old confronts an eight year old, it will be developmentally difficult for the younger child to receive the information in a healthy way. For instance, although sexually inappropriate behavior with a child is never acceptable, a sixteen year old may have more tools than a younger child to deal with such an event. A sixteen year old may observe and even comment on the inappropriateness of a remark or glance, but a younger child may simply be confused. An older child can use words and a larger body to set a boundary, or even to confront the unwanted action or words. A younger child may simply feel helpless or be seduced by kind words and deeds, especially if the child is alone or lonely.

Life consists of positive and negative events and memories. Together they make us human and give shape to our lives. We all go through stages, from being small humans in a confusing world to growing up and making sense of this world and our place in it. We create our identity and our sense of self though all these experiences.

Birth

From birth onward, a child is shaped by environment and family, as well as by personality and temperament. Development in early childhood was discussed in Chapter 11. From age three to five the child goes through separation and individuation, the development of healthy autonomy achieved by the right balance of closeness and separation. D. W. Winnicott, a developmental psychologist, called a caretaker who achieved this balance a "good-enough mother," meaning that children need good-enough nurturing, not perfection.

Early Childhood, Age 1 to 5
Home and security base

• Who was your major caretaker(s) during those years?

• What are your first memories before the age of five?

• Do you remember nature, landscape, your house, your room, your bed, a favorite toy or object, siblings, mother, father, grandparents?

• Did you live in the same house or apartment, town or city as extended family members?

Social world, friends, neighborhood

• Did you attend preschool or kindergarten?

• Did you have friends your own age? older? younger?

• What socioeconomic class did your family belong to during your early years?

• What do you remember about your neighborhood or your neighbors?

• How about the environment in which you grew up? What do you remember about landscape, weather, and location, such as farm, city, open space, mountains, ocean?

• What about experiences with nature or with awe and wonder?

• Were you exposed to any religious training, or did you have any spiritual experiences?

Family

• Name the people who surrounded you from birth to age five.

• What are the stories about you and who tells them?

• What myths do family members tell about you?
(She always . . . He never . . .)

• What have you heard about your early toilet training, eating habits, first teeth?

• What personality characteristic were you cherished for?

What trait that they found strange or disapproved of became part of the family lore?

Separations and disconnections

• Were you separated from your family during your first five years? Why?

• Did you move to a new place?

• Were you or your primary caretakers seriously ill?

• Were there wars or political upheavals, with relatives or parental figures going to war or leaving home?

• What do you know about your parents' and grandparents' attitudes regarding separations?

The School Years, Age 5 to 12

Friends and social life

• What kind of friends did you have? Were they older or younger, same or opposite sex?

• What did you like most and least about your friends?

• Were you accepted or a loner, shy or gregarious, a leader or follower?

• What do you understand about your attitude toward people, friends, closeness?

• What do you remember about yourself in relation to your peers at that time?

School days

• What was your attitude toward school and learning? Did you like it or dread it? Why?

• What were your favorite subjects? Do they have any bearing on your life now?

• What do you remember about your teachers? Who supported you or saw you as a good learner or person?

• Describe your school. What was it made of? Was it old, modern, clean, messy?

• How were the grades arranged?

• What techniques were used for teaching and learning?

• How did school affect you emotionally?

How did what happened at school integrate with home life?

Special training, such as music, sports, science, the arts

• How and when did you begin this special interest?

• Did you have a special teacher or mentor?

- What are your memories of these events?
- How did participating make you feel? Good, bad, or mixed?

Religious or spiritual training

- Did you attend services at a place of worship?
- What were you taught about a higher power?
- How did these teachings affect the life of the family at home?
- How did these teachings affect you privately?
- If you believed in a higher power, how did this belief affect your everyday life at school, home, or alone?

Your home

- What do you remember about your house?
- Describe your favorite rooms and the landscape surrounding your house.
- What do you remember about pets?
- Describe the family routine. Did you have chores?
- How were weekends different from the rest of the week?
- What was your neighborhood like?

Clothes

- What was your family's attitude toward appearance?
- How did your parents and grandparents dress?
- Did you wear what you wanted to?
- Did you feel proud or ashamed of your appearance?
- How do you think you looked compared to the other kids?

Discipline

- How did your parents use discipline or punishment with you and with your siblings?
- How were mistakes at school handled at home?
- Were you whipped or spanked? How do you define these terms?

- Were implements, such as spoons, belts, or switches, used to punish you?

- Were you yelled at or called names?

- Was humiliation used as a punishment technique?

- How did you feel about any punishment you received?

Play and creativity

- Were you encouraged to be a child or were you pushed to act older than your age? Were you allowed to play and daydream?

- Describe your play. What did you imagine in your play life?

- Did you keep your imaginative games a secret or share them?

- Did you draw or pay attention to your dreams and daydreams?

Adolescence, Age 13 to 19

Adolescence is a time to search for and find identity, often by rebelling against the norm, the family, and society. Certain aspects of the separation-individuation process of earlier years are repeated, and the adolescent reaches a new level of autonomy.

Sexuality and your body

- What was your family's attitude toward sex and physical closeness? Was it a healthy, open attitude or one of shame, guilt, and repression?

- Were your parents physically affectionate, or was sex repressed or absent in the house?

- When did you have "that talk" about sex and reproduction? Who talked to you, and what was his or her attitude?

- What did you think and feel about sex and reproduction?

- Did you date? As much or less than your friends?

- When you first went out on dates, how did you feel about yourself, your body, the date?

- How did you feel about your body changing? Did you feel guilty about sex, your body, masturbation?

• Did you talk about sex with your friends?

• What did you learn from them?

Friendship

• If you had a best friend, describe him or her.

• Were you social or a loner?

• Did you change your social and friendship habits from when you were younger, or did they stay the same?

• Did you like to spend time with the opposite sex or same sex friends?

• Did you ever feel confused about your own sexual identity?

• Did you have anyone you could talk to about this?

• How did your adolescent friendships help to shape you into the person you are now?

• What are some of your favorite memories from that phase of life when good friends mean so much?

School days

• Did your attitude toward school and learning change during adolescence?

• How did your life change when you began high school?

• Did you have a favorite teacher or mentor in high school? How did he or she affect your life?

• How did school affect you emotionally?

• How did what happened at school integrate with home life?

• How did you answer the question "What do you want to be when you grow up?"

• What did you think about growing up at this time?

• Did you look forward to it, dread it, worry about it, or not think about it at all?

Special training, such as music, sports, science, the arts

• What activities did you engage in and at what ages?

• What kind of self-esteem issues did the activities bring up for you?

• Write about your favorite memories of participating in these events.

• What are your worst memories?

• How did participating make you feel? Good, bad, or mixed?

• Did your family support your interests? If not, why not, as you understand it now and as you understood it then.

Religious and spiritual training

• Did your attendance at church or synagogue change during this period of your life? If so, how and why?

• How did you discuss your religious training with your parents, friends, and teachers? Did they talk about these things casually or formally, at dinner or by appointment, awkwardly or openly? Were you lectured at or listened to? Was religious training a choice or a requirement?

• Did you have mystical or inexplicable experiences, such as intuitive insights or premonitions?

• How did your family view death? What did you think about it?

• Had anyone in your family or circle of friends died by this point in your life?

• If you attended funerals or wakes, how did they affect you?

• How did you feel about cemeteries?

Clothes

• Were you allowed to wear the current fashions?

• How much did your parents control your clothes and style?

• Did you have the means to buy your own clothes?

• Could you trade with friends?

• Were you allowed to express your individuality through your appearance?

• For girls, how was the changing of your figure and the need for a bra or sanitary equipment handled? Who was in charge of that information and how was it delivered?

• Did you feel proud or ashamed of your appearance?

• How did you think you looked compared to the other kids?

• Were you proud or ashamed of the appearance of your family when friends came over?

Discipline

• When you were a teenager, how did your parents discipline or punish you and your siblings?

• How did mistakes at school get handled at home?

• Were you whipped or spanked? Were implements such as spoons, belts, or switches used? How did you feel about the punishment you received?

• Were you yelled at or called names?

• Was humiliation used as a punishment technique?

• If you were routinely punished, did you ever rebel and refuse to allow it any more? How did this refusal change your role or status in the family?

• How did you feel about this change in yourself and your relationship to your parents?

Leaving home

• How and at what age did you leave home? College, marriage, work, running away?

• Was your family prepared for this event? Or was there a family crisis about you or your siblings leaving home?

• How did you feel about leaving home?

Family rules, roles, and myths

• How did your family view itself? (As rich, poor, better than others, not as good as others?)

• Who was closest to you in your family? Who was closest to your parents?

• How was power defined in your family? Who had the most?

• During stress, did one person side with another? Was this pattern consistent or did the pairings change? Under what circumstances would this pairing occur? Did it happen frequently?

• How was your family like or unlike your parents' families?

• Is your extended family large or small?

Adult relationship with family of origin

• How were holidays handled when you left home?

• How did the family respond to your long-term relationship or marriage? Did they participate, send money, become over-involved, or maintain boundaries?

• How did you feel about going back home in your twenties, thirties, forties, and so forth?

What did you miss most after leaving home?

How are you like or unlike your family?

What generational patterns are you aware of?

Adult Life Stages

Courtship, partnership, marriage

• How did you feel about courtship and marriage?

• Why did you marry the person you married?

• How did your sexual orientation or identity affect your courtship and dating years?

Birth of children

• Did you want or welcome children?

• How did having children affect you, your identity, or how you lived your life?

• What was the best and worst aspect of having children?

• If you didn't have children but wanted them, how would your life have been different if you had had them?

• If you had them but didn't really want them, how do you feel about this now?

Work life and identity

• How did you answer the question "What do you want to be when you grow up" when you were 10, 20, 30, 40, 50?

• How would you answer it now?

• Who are you without work roles or work identity?

• Is there passion in your work life? A sense of accomplishment?

• What would you do when you got up in the morning if it were the last day of your life?

• What does money mean to you?

• If you had to choose, would you choose love over money or money over love?

• Does money bring security for you?

• If you could change your life, in what way would you do so?

Spiritual changes and development

• How do you define spirituality?

• How do you find spirituality in your life now?

• Describe the most spiritual experience you have ever had.

Appendix C

A Note to Therapists

The principles found in this book can help you expand and develop your therapeutic healing work with clients. Methods of using writing as a healing tool range from highly unstructured, free-form, or impressionistic imagery to small, selected, specific assignments in a logical fashion. The early Writing Invitations move gradually from less threatening, positive memories to stressful or traumatic ones. Like all therapy processes, writing can help to clarify and make more conscious the material clients need to explore. And as in other therapeutic interventions, issues such as compliance, resistance, and transference may occur, thus deepening, and perhaps complicating, the work.

The research by Pennebaker, Smyth, Klein, King, and others shows that writing can heal in a variety of ways—from digging deep into previous traumas to focusing on positive future goals and a best self. You must decide which technique is best for a particular client and his or her needs.

In general, if you're in doubt, ask the client to write about the positive first; avoid digging deep until the client has shown a willingness or ability to do that kind of work. Helpful Writing Invitations include writing about current positive experiences, or writing a fictional story based on the negative memory, and making it come out "right" by creating a better ending or changing the circumstances so the trauma does not take place. Writing a fairy tale, a mythic story that begins "once upon a time," offers a way to process material on various conscious and unconscious levels.

The techniques described in this book should be used with the understanding that the more fragile the client, the more structure is needed. Writing brings chaos into form, but confronting specific details and having a grounded perception about certain traumas can be too intense for clients at early stages of the work. Using freewriting or journal writing can be too open-ended and unstructured, subjecting a fragile client to feeling overwhelmed by a flood of memories and perceptions.

Writer as Witness

Writing true stories is powerful because it allows the writer to encounter and witness former selves, and to integrate these selves into a current view of the ego by another aspect of the self. The writer observes himself as a child, adolescent, young adult, and relives his life choices, changes, and roads not taken. As the self goes back and forth between different perceptual windows, the ego is woven into a tapestry of greater strength, confidence, and understanding. That new perspective develops further if the writer creates a lengthy work over time. Each draft creates another level of understanding. A finished memoir is a powerful testament to survival and the triumph of creativity over depression and woundedness.

Memoir-as-witnessing performs an important healing function. Alice Miller's work provides a context for understanding the idea of therapist as witness. Memoir writing extends this witnessing into the realm of creativity and imagination. The arts have long been understood to be a mode of healing and self-expression that transcends pain and suffering.

Writing Assignments

To ensure the best results, ask clients to write in a journal about a specific, agreed-upon topic arising from the session or selected together from the many Writing Invitations in this book. If you already know your clients well, you will be aware of topics that might trigger a strong reaction and be able to guide them into that material when they are ready for it. I have often had clients read their writing to me in session, which provides a focus and support for the writing process. Also, because compliance can be an issue with assignments, if clients expect you to ask them to read during their sessions, they are more likely to do the writing.

Before assigning a particular topic, you'll want to assess your clients to make sure they have the requisite ego strength to explore and write about trauma in depth. Therapeutic concerns about re-traumatization need to be taken into account. Pennebaker did not find this to be a problem in his early studies, but his experimental population was not clinical. In the context of ongoing depth therapy, you might find more vulnerability to regression in your clients as a result of writing about areas that are too raw. If you have any doubt about how far a client should go into uncharted traumatic territory, err on the side of caution.

You may choose to create your own writing-therapy plan with each client, beginning with simple, positive stories. To assess what kinds of stories you might assign, you will need to know the client well. The developmental questionnaire in this book can be used to help assess the level of story, or trauma, the client may not yet have reached through therapy. You will discover your client's hot spots and be able to suggest an appropriate writing plan.

Clients who are not ready to examine their own life might write about other family members or conduct genealogical research in preparation for writing about the family's history. Safe writing subjects include landscape, weather, the history of the place where the family made its home, and a chronicle of the times in which the family lived. Such clients should enter the territory of memory gradually, exploring history and digging up clues. The missing pieces of the story and unanswered questions become subjects for investigation in the search for identity and self-history. This kind of writing helps to resolve questions about the family of origin and provides a way to do family therapy with one person, a technique commonly used by family therapists.

Together, you and your client can design a special notebook or journal. At the top of each page or two, list the Writing Invitations you have chosen. This way, the client knows what to expect and can be thinking about the next writing exercise. Such a planned structure helps the client use writing as a gentle healing process.

As anyone who writes knows, however, writing can "accidentally" lead into unexpected and surprising terrain. An unconscious moat is breached, and new territory opens up. As the therapist, you would either need to extend the range of therapy into this new territory or back up the work until the client is fully ready to face it. These accidental incursions help break through invisible walls. Imposing a structure lessens the possibility of accidental breakthroughs, but there is no guarantee that they won't occur.

Writing is not always an appropriate intervention, but it can be added at appropriate junctures in the therapy. Most clients do benefit from therapeutic writing. Adding bibliotherapy can create an atmosphere of open exploration into ideas, fictional worlds, and character types that help clients explore denied aspects of self or that show how other families cope with problems. Reading published poetry, fiction, biographies, autobiographies, and memoirs can have a powerful effect by giving clients the sense that they are not alone as they heal, or by allowing them to identify with others who have had similar problems. See the list of published memoirs at the end of this book.

Research showing that writing helps heal diseases such as asthma, chronic fatigue syndrome, and even heart disease provides us therapists with more support and validation for using bibliotherapy and writing therapy as part of our arsenal of tools. We do not have to be writers ourselves to offer these techniques; and we can support clients in writing not for a result or a grade but for the joy and satisfaction of self-expression. In this way, the client's identity develops, with old roles and patterns seen as part of another self, the old self that is being shed, like a chrysalis, for a new one.

A Four-Tiered Approach to Therapeutic Writing

1. The Past in the Family

a. Help the client use the timeline to sort out possible stories, to determine the context of his family's life, and to figure out which stories need to be written.

b. Choose a small number of positive family stories. Ask the client to write one each week or month. The pace will be determined by you and the client.

c. If the client says there are no positive stories, have her write about how she wishes she had lived. Ask her to create a fictional life with positive outcomes.

d. Create a genogram to sort out family dynamics.

e. Use the genogram to examine patterns in the current generation.

f. Ask the client to write about the insights gained in the process of doing these Writing Invitations.

2. The Present Self

a. Ask the client to keep a journal or diary to record the present self, writing in an unstructured, free-flowing manner about current states of mind, goals, and problems. This approach is useful for those clients who do not need the structure of specific Writing Invitations.

b. Have the client explore the physical, emotional, intellectual, and spiritual self through writing.

c. Ask the client to keep a dream journal.

d. Spiritual autobiography or journeys into memory can guide the client through deep internal reflection and exploration of self.

e. Reflective Writing Invitations, such as writing answers to the question "Who Am I," help focus on identity resolution and the development of the real self. A new "Who Am I" story could be written every week or month.

3. The Past Self

a. Focusing on the past self or selves deepens the work and provides the possibility of integration. The past family history, the past self, and how the current self is on the way to becoming the future self can all be written about in an ongoing memoir.

4. The Future Self

a. The goal is to help the client envision a new life, a healed self, and a positive way to integrate his new learning. You can structure various Writing Invitations that connect to the work the client has already completed and to the life story you have come to know. Some useful questions include:

    i. Who am I becoming?
    ii. Who do I want to become?
    iii. What is the best self I can be?
    iv. What transformations do I want to make in my life?

Writing therapy gives a client another way to express her hidden self and to reveal the beautiful person she is within. Miraculous changes can happen through writing. These changes occur slowly. And they may remain invisible in the client's psyche and in the depths of his or her soul.

To learn more about the studies on writing as healing, read *Opening Up: The Healing Power of Expressing Emotions* by James Pennebaker. *The Writing Cure*, edited by Stephen Lepore and Joshua Smyth, with a last chapter by Pennebaker, includes more recent studies and continues the work of the earlier researchers exploring such questions as whether writing affects the healing process of diseases, whether positive writing has as salutary an effect as writing about pain and trauma, and how writing affects memory. Some of the studies show that positive writing about the future is as healing as writing about trauma.

As a therapist, you can use autobiographical writing as an adjunct to your therapeutic work to create awareness of family stories, to knit together the client's fragmented story, and to strengthen the client's identity and sense of relatedness to others. The client learns that a self-history carries within it wisdom about life and family, and that story is a way to create a new future as well as to heal the past.

❋

Appendix D

Quick Reminders for When You Think You're Stuck

- Keep writing. Writing leads to more writing.
- Freewrite in a journal even if you aren't able to write a particular story.
- Read other memoirs to learn more about the writing process, style, and language.
- Outline, edit, and tinker with other stories when you aren't in the mood to write a new one.
- Go on the Internet to look at other people's writing and sites that encourage writing.
- Get out the photos, and look at the people and times you're writing about.
- Write a one- or two-page portrait of a family member or mentor who has helped you.
- Write a quick sketch of a happy moment.
- List the blessings in your life.
- Read fiction for style, technique, plot, scene, and character development tips.
- Eavesdrop in cafés, listening to dialogue and speech cadences.
- Read poetry.
- Attend author events and readings for inspiration.

© 2007 by Linda Joy Myers

References

Adams, Kathleen. 1990. *Journal to the Self.* New York: Warner Books.

———. 1998. *The Way of the Journal.* Lutherville, MD: The Sidran Press.

———. 2000. *The Write Way to Wellness.* Lakewood, CO: Center for Journal Therapy.

Albert, Susan Wittig. 1997. *Writing from Life: Telling Your Soul's Story.* New York: Jeremy P. Tarcher/Putnam.

Allende, Isabel. 1985. *The House of the Spirits.* New York: Knopf.

Allison, Dorothy. 1992. *Bastard Out of Carolina.* New York: Dutton.

Baldwin, Christina. 1998. *Life's Companion: Journal Writing as a Spiritual Quest.* New York: Bantam Doubleday Dell.

Bachelard, Paul. 1994. Reprint. *The Poetics of Space.* Boston: Beacon Press. Original edition, New York: Orion Press, 1964.

Black, Claudia. 1981. *It Will Never Happen to Me.* New York: Ballantine Books.

Brande, Dorothea. [1943] 1981. *Becoming a Writer.* Reprint, with a foreword by John Gardner, New York: Jeremy P. Tarcher/Putnam.

Cameron, Julia. 2002. 10th anniversary edition. *The Artist's Way: A Spiritual Path to Higher Creativity.* New York: Jeremy P. Tarcher/Putnam.

Chandler, Marilyn. 1990. *A Healing Art: Regeneration Through Autobiography.* New York: Garland Publishing.

Conroy, Pat. 1986. *The Prince of Tides.* New York: Houghton Mifflin.

DeSalvo, Louise. 2000. *Writing as a Way of Healing: How Telling Our Stories Transforms Our Lives.* Boston: Beacon Press.

Dillard, Annie. 1987. To Fashion a Text. In *Inventing the Truth: The Art and Craft of Memoir,* edited and with a memoir and introduction by William Zinsser. Boston: Houghton Mifflin.

Engel, Susan. 1999. *Context is Everything: The Nature of Memory.* New York: W. H. Freeman & Co.

Fox, John. 1997. *Poetic Medicine.* New York: Jeremy P. Tarcher/Putnam.

Glickstein, Lee. 1999. *Be Heard Now! Tap into Your Inner Speaker and Communicate with Ease.* Reprint. New York: Broadway Books.

Herman, Judith. 1992. *Trauma and Recovery.* New York: Basic Books.

Hanh, Thich Nhat. 1997. *Teachings on Love.* Berkeley, CA: Parallax Press.

Hoffman, Bob. 1976. *Getting Divorced from Mom and Dad.* New York: E. P. Dutton.

King, Laurie. 2002. Gain Without Pain? Expressive Writing and Self-Regulation. In *The Writing Cure: How Expressive Writing Promotes Health and Emotional Well-Being,* eds., Stephen J. Lepore and Joshua M. Smyth. Washington, D.C.: American Psychological Association.

Lamott, Anne. 1995. *Bird by Bird: Some Instructions on Writing and Life.* New York: Pantheon Books.

Ledoux, Denis. 1991. *Turning Memories into Memoirs.* Lisbon Falls, ME: Soleil Press.

Leffland, Ella. 1985. Reprint. *Rumors of Peace.* New York: HarperCollins.

Lepore, Stephen J., and Joshua M. Smyth, eds. 2002. *The Writing Cure: How Expressive Writing Promotes Health and Emotional Well-Being.* Washington, D.C.: American Psychological Association.

Levine, Peter A. 1997. *Waking the Tiger: Healing Trauma.* Berkeley, CA: North Atlantic Books.

Lopez, Judith. 2001. *Immune Dysfunction: Winning My Battle Against Toxins, Illness & the Medical Establishment.* Mill Valley,

CA: Millpond Press.

Mahler, Margaret. 1975. *The Psychological Birth of the Human Infant*. New York: Basic Books.

Masterson, James. 1988. *The Real Self*. New York: The Free Press.

Merton, Thomas. 1999. 50th anniversary edition. *The Seven Storey Mountain*. New York: Harcourt Brace.

Metzger, Deena. 1992. *Writing for Your Life*. New York: HarperCollins.

Miller, Alice, 2001. *The Truth Will Set You Free*. New York: Basic Books.

Myers, Linda Joy 2005. *Don't Call Me Mother: Breaking the Chain of Mother-Daughter Abandonment*. Berkeley, CA: Two Bridges Press.

Nin, Anais. 1967. *The Diary of Anais Nin*. Vol. II (March 1937). New York: Swallow Press.

Pennebaker, James W. 1990. *Opening Up: The Healing Power of Expressing Emotions*. New York: The Guilford Press.

————. 2002. Personal conversation with author, February 4, in Austin, TX.

Pennebaker, James W., and Janel D. Seagal. 1999. Forming a Story: The Health Benefits of Narrative. *Journal of Clinical Psychology* 55(10):1243–1254.

Price, Reynolds. 1994. *A Whole New Life*. New York: Plume.

Rainer, Tristine. 1997. *The New Diary: Your Life as Story*. New York: Jeremy P. Tarcher/Putnam.

————. 1998. *Your Life as Story: Discovering the "New Autobiography" and Writing Memoir as Literature*. New York: Jeremy P. Tarcher/Putnam.

Reichl, Ruth. 1999. *Tender at the Bone: Growing Up at the Table*. New York: Broadway Books.

Rothschild, Babette. 2000. *The Body Remembers: The Psychophysiology of Trauma and Trauma Treatment*. New York: W. W. Norton & Co.

Salon.com. http://www.salon.com/books/feature/2001/12/12/lauck/print.html. Accessed 6/28/02.

Smyth, J., A. Stone, A. Hurewitz, and A. Kaell. 1999. Writing about stressful events produces symptom reduction in asthmatics and rheumatoid arthritics: a randomized trial. *Journal of the American Medical Association*, 281, 1304–1309.

Suzuki, Shunryu. 1973. *Zen Mind, Beginner's Mind.* New York: Weatherhill.

Tan, Amy. 1994. *The Joy Luck Club.* New York: Prentice Hall.

Thomas, Lewis. 1974. *The Lives of a Cell.* New York: Viking Press.

Ueland, Brenda. 1987. *If You Want to Write: A Book about Art, Independence and Spirit.* St. Paul, MN: Graywolf Press.

Wakefield, Dan. 1990. *The Story of Your Life: Writing a Spiritual Autobiography.* Boston: Beacon Press.

Weldon, Michele 2001. *Writing To Save Your Life.* Hazelden. Center City, MI.

Woolf, Virginia. [1927] 1989. *To the Lighthouse.* New York: Harvest Books.

About the Author

*D*r. Linda Joy Myers, prize-winning author of *Don't Call Me Mother: Breaking the Chain of Mother Daughter Abandonment*, has been a therapist in Berkeley, California for over twenty-five years. Through her classes and workshops, online memoir coaching, and speaking engagements nationwide, Linda teaches the powerful healing process of writing our true stories.

Her first book *Becoming Whole: Writing Your Healing Story* is used as a text by many therapists, ministers, and writing coaches. Linda tends three children, three grandchildren, an assortment of cats, and a rose garden. She is currently at work on her first novel.

Please visit Linda at: www.memories and memoirs.com